Learn to Code Curriculum Guide
with Dash & Dot
K-5

Credits & Acknowledgements

Producer: June Lin
Editors: Charlotte Cheng, April Crane
Curriculum Guide Author: Charlotte Cheng
Challenge Card Authors: Charlotte Cheng, Katie Chirhart, Kathryn Staton
Lesson Authors: Katie Chirhart, Julia Dweck, Julie Goo, Katrina Keene
Illustration: Dag Haile
Design: Chris Cast, Desiree Jue, Lucy Wang
Education Team at Wonder Workshop: Mike Lorion, Naomi Harm, Bryan Miller, Dylan Portelance, Hetav Sanghavi, Darri Stephens, Amy Wilson

Wonder Workshop, Inc.
1500 Fashion Island Blvd., #200
San Mateo, CA 94404, USA

Support:
help.makewonder.com
support@makewonder.com

Copyright @ 2017 Wonder Workshop, Inc.
All Rights Reserved. Wonder Workshop, Inc. reserves the right to amend or improve the product design, application software, and/or user guide without any restriction or obligation to notify users.

Designed in California. Made in China. Imported and distributed by Wonder Workshop, Inc.

Library of Congress Cataloging-in-Publication Data available.

ISBN: 978-0-9989850-1-5

Table of Contents

Teaching Coding with Robotics.. 2

Wonder Workshop Robots and Apps.. 4

Setting Up Your Classroom.. 6

Learn to Code Curriculum.. 8

Lesson Plans... 9

Challenge Cards.. 10

Assessment Strategies.. 13

Implementation Options... 16

Best Practices.. 20

Challenge Card Solutions... 24

Appendix... 170

    Tips and Tricks Handout... 171

    K-2 Planning Worksheet for Dash.. 172

    K-2 Planning Worksheet for Dot.. 173

    3-5 Planning Worksheet.. 174

    Challenge Card Checklists... 175

    Blockly Puzzle Tracker.. 178

    Reflections Worksheet.. 180

    Advanced Reflections Worksheet... 181

    Challenge Card Template.. 182

    Troubleshooting Handout.. 183

    Problem Solving & Debugging Handout.................................... 184

    Evaluation Rubric.. 185

Glossary.. 186

Welcome to the world of coding and robotics with Wonder Workshop!

We're excited that you've chosen our robots, Dash and Dot, for your classroom. When used with our apps, Dash and Dot bring coding and STEM to life in a collaborative, interactive, and intuitive way!

In this guide, you will learn about **Wonder Workshop's Learn to Code Curriculum**, including: how to use our robots and curriculum content, implementation strategies, project-based assessment strategies, and cross-curricular extensions.

Teaching Coding with Robotics

Why Coding?

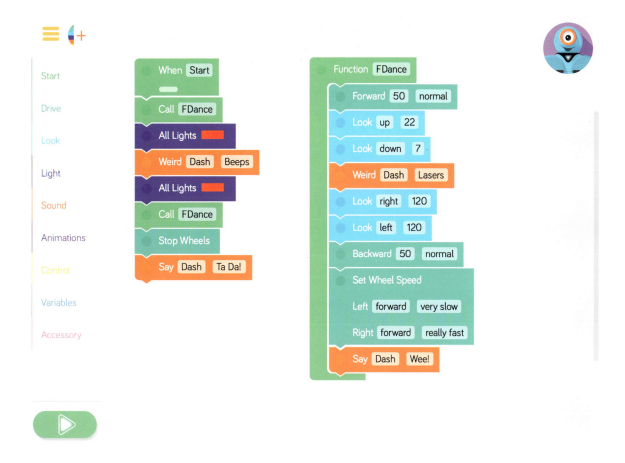

Learning to code helps students develop essential 21st-century skills.

Through coding, students learn to see the world through the lens of computational thinking. **Computational thinking** enables students to decompose problems, recognize patterns, and understand abstract concepts. Students can apply these skills to their everyday lives.

Coding is also a new type of literacy that prepares students for the careers of tomorrow. Whether it's a career in graphic arts or financial consulting, more and more occupations require employees to have at least a fundamental understanding of reading and writing code. Coding also prepares students for successful and high-demand careers in STEM (Science, Technology, Engineering, and Mathematics).

Why Robotics?

Robots are an integral part of students' everyday lives. From doing chores with a robo vacuum to buying a snack at a vending machine, robots are everywhere around them.

A **robot** is a machine that can gather information about its environment and use that information and any pre-programmed instructions to complete tasks. Robots are controlled by code to perform these instructions. These could be very simple and specific, like completing a set of movements that would cut a piece of wood to a certain length, or extremely complex, like teaching the robot how to respond in new situations.

Robotics brings coding and STEM to life. It provides great opportunities for students to develop and apply their coding skills through hands-on experiences. Dash and Dot provide students with instant feedback and engages their spatial awareness capabilities. With lights, sounds, and movement, Dash and Dot help students see how they can solve problems and express ideas through the power of code!

Our Products

Dash and Dot

Dash and Dot are smart robots for curious minds. Their personalities come alive with animations, sounds, and lights to engage students' creativity. These clever and rugged robots come equipped with speakers, sensors, microphones, lights, and motors that allow students to explore the world of robotics in a creative and interactive way.

If this is your first time experiencing Dash and Dot, you can learn more about our robots here: education.makewonder.com/professional-development

For **troubleshooting** and **FAQs**, you can also check our help page here: help.makewonder.com

Our Apps

We offer five free apps which give students the opportunity to experience coding in a scaffolded manner. Go, Xylo, and Path are designed for pre-readers, while Blockly and Wonder offer more advanced programming platforms for older students.

With Blockly, students learn to code using a block-based programming tool. Many students have exposure to block-based programming through ScratchJr or Code.org. Thus, Blockly is a great way to introduce robotics as students can program Dash and Dot using a language that is familiar to them.

With Wonder, students use a revolutionary, flow-based programming language, where they arrange their code into patterns that are similar to flowcharts or decision trees. With this type of programming, students create state machines which is similar to what robotics engineers use in their work.

You can learn more about our variety of apps on our website: education.makewonder.com

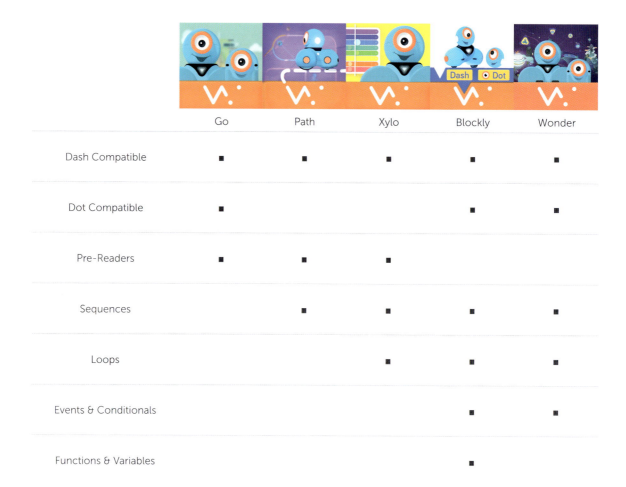

	Go	Path	Xylo	Blockly	Wonder
Dash Compatible	■	■	■	■	■
Dot Compatible	■			■	■
Pre-Readers	■	■	■		
Sequences		■	■	■	■
Loops			■	■	■
Events & Conditionals				■	■
Functions & Variables				■	

Setting Up Your Classroom

Robots, Apps, and Tablets

Our **Learn to Code Curriculum** works best if students have access to both Dash and Dot robots. We recommend assigning 2–3 students per robot. In small groups, students can share their ideas, take turns, and work together to complete challenges with Dash and Dot.

Before introducing Dash and Dot to the classroom, be sure to:

☐ Individually name each robot.

☐ Use masking tape and/or a marker to label the robots with their names.

☐ Fully charge each robot.

☐ Fully charge and label each tablet (e.g., "Tablet #1, Tablet #2").

☐ Download the Blockly app onto each tablet.

☐ Go through the setup process in the Blockly app and give each robot the name you labeled the robot with.

☐ Create floorspace for each group's robot and materials. To use our **Challenge Cards**, we usually recommend providing at least a 4 x 4 sq. ft. space for each robot.

To help student groups keep track of their work, make sure each group always uses the same tablet and saves their work within Blockly.

You can find **setup**, **care**, and **maintenance** tutorials for our robots here: education.makewonder.com/professional-development

Additional Materials

Some of our lessons and challenges require students to use additional materials to complete the challenges.

We recommend that you have the following materials available in the classroom:

- paper or plastic cups (3 per group)

- thick books or blocks (4–6 per group)

- painter's or masking tape (1 roll per group)

- rulers (1 per group)

- small toys/objects (3 per group)

- **Bulldozer** accessory (1 per group)

- 4ft x 6ft (128cm x 180cm) gridded mat or **Wonder Workshop** mat (1 per group)

For additional robots, accessories, gridded mats, and card sets, you can shop at our online store: store.makewonder.com

Making It Work

We recognize that classrooms have different limitations and encourage you to be creative with the resources you have!

If you are missing either Dash or Dot, many of our Dot challenges can be completed with Dash and vice versa. You can also adjust the challenge objectives.

If you are missing some of the materials, encourage students to use alternative resources. For example, students can create their own bulldozer using LEGO™ bricks and our **Building Brick Connectors**. Students can also create coordinate grids on the floor using a ruler and painter's tape.

Learn to Code Scope and Sequence

In our **Learn to Code Curriculum**, we outline a recommended action plan for integrating coding and robotics into your daily practices.

This plan offers a variety of teaching tools that include lesson plans, in-app content, student-facing challenge cards, a solution guide, and authentic assessments.

Our **Learn to Code Curriculum** is organized into 6 coding levels: A through F. Similar to Code.org's **Computer Science (CS) Fundamentals** series, each coding level covers two or three of the six fundamental coding concepts: sequences, loops, events, conditionals, functions, and variables.

You can learn more about Code.org's **CS Fundamentals** series here: https://code.org/educate/curriculum/elementary-school

Our Scope and Sequence

Our scope & sequence progresses students through the fundamentals of coding concepts.

Level	A	B	C	D	E	F
Recommended Grade Level	Kindergarten	1st Grade	2nd Grade	3rd Grade	4th Grade	5th Grade
Sequences	Sequences	Sequences with Parameters	Sequences with Complex Parameters	Practice	Practice	Practice
Loops	Repeat Forever	Repeat Forever, Repeat X Times	Multiple Loops	Nested	Repeat Until	Practice
Events		Wait for Event	Event Handlers (1 robot)	Event Handlers (2 robots)	Practice	Practice
Conditionals				If/Then	If/Else	Nested
Functions					Functions	Practice
Variables						Variables

For students who are new to using Dash and Dot, we recommend beginning at Coding Level A. Each coding level is aligned to a recommended grade as a guide, but we also suggest that you consider your students' coding experience when determining where to start. The coding levels spiral and scaffold to build upon skills learned in previous lessons.

Lesson Plans

Our 30 free lesson plans (six per coding level) are available online at:
 education.makewonder.com/curriculum

These lesson plans include the following elements:

- **Warm Up:** Connect to students' prior coding knowledge with introductory exercises

- **Direct Instruction:** Introduce new coding concepts through modeling and demonstrations

- **Guided Practice:** Guide students through in-app puzzles and preset programs, primarily found in our free Blockly app

- **Independent Practice:** Have students complete sets of three student-facing **Challenge Cards** and in-app extension activities

- **Wrap Up:** Close the lesson with student presentations and/or wrap-up discussions

The lessons are designed to meet Computer Science Teacher Association (CSTA) standards and International Society for Technology in Education (ISTE) Student Standards. More information about these standard correlations can be found within each lesson plan.

Challenge Cards

Unique to our **Learn to Code Curriculum**, is the set of 72 physical **Challenge Cards** that students use for independent practice. The cards follow a sequence within and across the lessons that progresses students through each coding level's programming concepts.

Anatomy of a Challenge Card

The **Challenge Cards** are designed to engage students independently or collaboratively in small groups. Help your students become familiar with the important elements on each card. This guidance will enable them to determine which robots and materials they'll need for each challenge.

Coding Concepts

Lists the main concept that students will be practicing (not including Bonus content). Concepts include: **sequencing**, **loops**, **events**, **conditionals**, **functions**, **variables**.

Coding Level

Indicates the card's coding level (A-F)

Illustration

An engaging illustration of Dash and/or Dot helps jump-start students' imaginations.

Story

The story gives students a reason to complete the challenge. Examples include:

- Help Dash/Dot accomplish something.
- Have Dash/Dot help someone.
- Use Dash/Dot in a game that students can play with friends.

Side 1 of each challenge card engages students through creative stories and objectives.

10

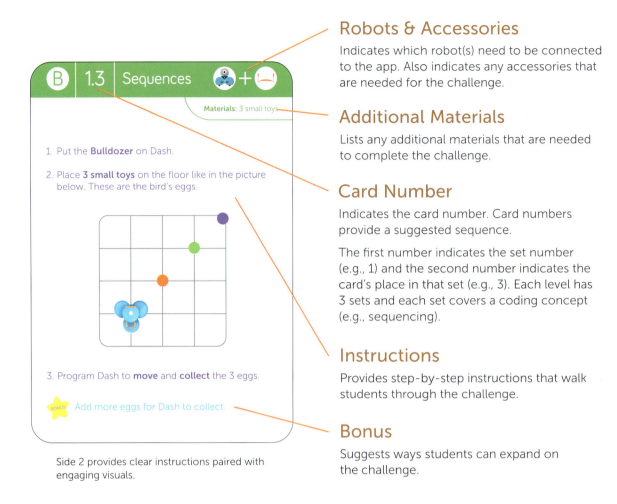

Side 2 provides clear instructions paired with engaging visuals.

Robots & Accessories
Indicates which robot(s) need to be connected to the app. Also indicates any accessories that are needed for the challenge.

Additional Materials
Lists any additional materials that are needed to complete the challenge.

Card Number
Indicates the card number. Card numbers provide a suggested sequence.

The first number indicates the set number (e.g., 1) and the second number indicates the card's place in that set (e.g., 3). Each level has 3 sets and each set covers a coding concept (e.g., sequencing).

Instructions
Provides step-by-step instructions that walk students through the challenge.

Bonus
Suggests ways students can expand on the challenge.

NOTE: You can find comprehensive solutions for each of the 72 Challenge Cards in the Challenge Card Solutions section of this guide.

Challenge Tips and Tricks

Here are several tips and tricks that you can share with your students as they complete our **Challenge Cards**:

- **Determine team roles:** Swap roles with your teammates for each challenge. Team roles include lead programmer, robot wrangler, and documentarian.

- **Plan your path:** Use your finger or a pencil and paper to draw out the path you want Dash to follow. Use that path to help you plan out the sequencing of the blocks you'll need in Blockly. You can also test a possible solution by getting up and walking the path that you think Dash should take.

- **Mark your key spots:** Use masking or painter's tape to mark Dash's starting spot and the location of any obstacles/objects that are part of the challenge (in case they move).

- **Go back to start:** Always put Dash back at the starting spot before playing a program again.

- **Use the When Start block:** Place your blocks under the **When Start** block. The **When Start** block should always be on your screen.

Think in centimeters: Dash moves in centimeters. A centimeter is about the width of your finger.

Check off the steps: Use a dry erase marker to check off each step as you complete it. Make sure you erase the marks after you're done with the **Challenge Card**.

Help your robots hear you: If the classroom is noisy, use the **Hear Clap** cue instead of the **Hear Voice** cue. You can also ask the teacher for permission to try out your program with Dash and/or Dot outside or in the hallway.

Up the challenge: Set a time limit for yourself or your team.

NOTE: Find the **Tips and Tricks Handout** in the **Appendix** of this guide.

Assessment Strategies

Wonder Journals

We recommend providing an authentic assessment by having students create a **Wonder Journal**. In this journal, students can document their design process, capture their program solutions, and reflect on their coding experiences.

CSTA, ISTE, NGSS, and Common Core standards all value the importance of having students reflect on their learning process. When students reflect on their work, they're able to:

- identify their strengths and weaknesses.

- assess and learn from their mistakes.

- improve their work through iterative design thinking.

- identify any resources, guidance, or support they may need.

- create an informed plan for their next projects.

Wonder Journals can also become portfolios that allow students to share the programs they've created and demonstrate what they've learned to their friends and family!

Wonder Journals can include:

Planning Worksheets

Students can use our **Planning Worksheets** to map out the steps they'll need to complete each challenge. Their plans can include diagrams, references to specific blocks, or flowcharts.
NOTE: Find our multi-level **Planning Worksheets** in the **Appendix** of this guide.

Screenshots

After students complete each challenge or project, have them take a screenshot of their Blockly code. Then, you can compare their programs to the suggested solutions we've provided in this guide. If needed, demonstrate for your class how to take screenshots with your classroom's tablets.

Challenge Card Checklists

As students work through the **Challenge Cards**, have them use our **Challenge Card Checklists** to track their progress. You can then use these checklists to identify the students who need more support or guidance. These checklists can also be used to group students at different coding levels.

NOTE: Find our **Challenge Card Checklists** in the **Appendix** of this guide.

Blockly Puzzle Tracker

As students work through puzzles in Blockly, have them use our **Blockly Puzzle Tracker** to track their progress so they know which puzzle to return to or try next.

NOTE: Find our **Blockly Puzzle Tracker** in the **Appendix** of this guide.

Videos

Students can also take videos of Dash and Dot while running their programs. In this way, they can showcase any custom sounds or light patterns they've recorded. Additionally, the videos allow you to assess whether their programs completely meet each challenge's objectives.

Reflection Worksheets

Students can use our **Reflection Worksheets** to record their results, identify any struggles, and reflect on what they've learned. Have younger students record their thoughts using drawings and diagrams. Encourage older students to use coding and scientific vocabulary in their observations (e.g., observations, results, functions, variables, algorithms).

NOTE: Find our multi-level **Reflection Worksheets** in the **Appendix** of this guide.

Digital Portfolio Platforms

Digital portfolio platforms may help students assemble the different elements of their **Wonder Journal.** With these platforms they can:

- Share screenshots of their code.
- Take videos of their robots in action.
- Write reflections about their coding experiences.
- Give feedback to each other.
- Share **Wonder Journals** with friends and family.

Here are a few digital portfolio platforms that pair well with our curriculum:

Seesaw

Seesaw offers various account sign-in options that provide easy access for all K–12 students, including pre-readers and those without email addresses.

Seesaw also includes features like voice recording and mark-up tools for students to reflect on their work.

OneNote

OneNote's Class Notebook allows you to create digital journals for each student, assign specific tasks to different students, and provide individualized feedback.

Class Notebook also enables students to collaboratively embed videos, photos, and voice recording into a group journal.

Google Classroom

Google Classroom is a great way for student groups to collaborate on a journal together. Multiple students can work on a document and provide feedback at the same time.

Google Classroom allows students to organize their entries and multimedia files into folders. These folders and files can then be shared with specific students, groups, teachers, and family members.

Evaluation

To evaluate the **Wonder Journals**, you can use:

Our Rubric

Share the rubric with students before they begin coding so that the entire classroom is aware of your learning and performance expectations. Then use the rubric to evaluate each student's portfolio. We think that life skills, such as communication and collaboration, are just as important as coding skills. Thus, we have incorporated assessment criteria for both academic and life skills into our rubric system. We also encourage you to adapt the rubric to meet your students' needs.

NOTE: Find our **Evaluation Rubric Handout** in the **Appendix** of this guide.

Peer Review

Peer review is an important practice that is commonly used in diverse work environments. Your students can practice peer review with Dash and Dot, too. They can use our rubric to assess each other's programs and portfolios and provide constructive feedback.

We recommend that you review best practices for giving and receiving feedback with your class. These strategies include:

- Give one compliment and one suggestion.

- Be kind and considerate when giving feedback.

- Use concrete details and examples when giving suggestions.

- Explain why you like or don't like something about your classmate's program.

- Listen and write down the feedback you receive.

- Spend time to think how you can incorporate the feedback into your next program

Implementation Options

We designed our **Learn to Code Curriculum** and **Challenge Cards** to accommodate different classroom structures. This way, you can easily adapt the curriculum to meet the specific needs of your class.

Whole-Class Instruction

Whole-class instruction is a great way to introduce coding to younger students.

Use a projector to share your tablet screen with the class. Then work through our lessons together as a class. Have student volunteers take turns helping you walk through in-app puzzles and preset program extensions. Encourage students to explain their thinking when they share coding decisions.

Introduce the **Challenge Cards** to the students by completing each challenge together as a whole class. Then, divide the students into small groups and have them work together to complete the challenges again. This repetition not only provides individual, hands-on practice, but since each card allows for variations on the solution, students can personalize their own programs with custom light or sound blocks.

Once students are familiar with Blockly and the **Challenge Cards**, they'll be able to work more independently in future sessions and develop the flexibility to progress at their own pace.

Differentiated Instruction with Small Groups

If your students have a wide range of coding abilities, you can form groups based on their coding levels. Refer to students' **Challenge Card Checklists** to assign each group the set of cards that best matches their coding level. Then student groups can work collaboratively on their card sets, advancing at their own pace, while you facilitate and provide support as needed via our lesson plan content.

Learning Centers

Our **Learn to Code Curriculum** is also perfect for learning centers. Set up a **Wonder Workshop** learning center with Dash and Dot robots, tablets, a set of **Challenge Cards**, and any additional materials that students may need (e.g., rulers, masking tape).

You can use our lesson plans to introduce new coding concepts or strategies at the beginning of each class and then let students rotate through the Wonder Workshop learning center. Students then can progress through the cards at their own pace.

Wonder App Extensions

While our Blockly app lets students program using a block-based language, our Wonder app enables students to program in a completely different way.

With the Wonder app, students use a flow-based language in which they arrange their code into patterns that are similar to flowcharts or decision trees.

Advanced coders improve their coding abilities by learning multiple programming languages. As your more advanced students complete challenges in Blockly, have them try to complete the same challenges in Wonder.

For example, for card A 3.3:

The Blockly solution would look something like this:

While the Wonder solution would look something like this:

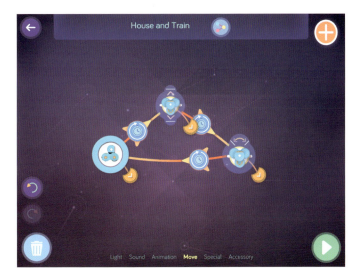

Students can walk through the Wonder app's Scroll Quest to get accustomed to programming in a flow-based language.

Then, they can compare and contrast Blockly and Wonder's coding languages. Encourage them to answer questions such as:

- Which challenges are easier with the Blockly app, and why?

- Which challenges are easier with the Wonder app, and why?

- If you could design **Challenge Cards** for Wonder, what would they look like? What would be different from and what would be the same as the cards designed for Blockly?

Design Your Own Challenge

Another fun extension activity is to have students design their own challenges. Students can attempt to complete each other's challenges and give feedback to one another. This helps them practice their instructional writing skills and explore coding concepts in a different way.

NOTE: Students can use our blank **Challenge Card Template** which can be found in the **Appendix** of this guide.

Best Practices

Dash and Dot work best in student-centered coding environments. These environments establish a classroom culture where students take control of their own learning process! Here are a few suggestions for creating a student-centered coding environment in your own classroom:

Learn with Your Students

Technology is constantly changing and adapting to new platforms. You shouldn't feel as though you need to know everything about coding and robotics before you introduce them to the class. Don't be afraid to explore Blockly and Dash and Dot along with your students. As you learn about new coding concepts together, you're able to model good learning practices such as finding answers and solutions through experimentation and trial and error.

Growth Mindset

In coding, students progress more quickly and effectively when they learn from their own mistakes. If students are afraid to fail, they are less likely to discover innovative ideas and designs. Encourage your students to try out different strategies as they work on the Challenge Cards. Remind them to see their mistakes as progress and growth, and encourage them to "fail fast and fail forward!"

Collaboration

As mentioned before, Dash and Dot are best explored in small groups of 2–3 students. By working in groups, students get to practice 21st-century skills such as collaboration, communication, and cooperation. These essential life skills are constantly required and practiced in modern-day work environments.

Encourage students to share the tablets and robots. Have them establish and rotate through roles such as:

- lead programmer: holds the tablet and integrates group member ideas to create the program in Blockly

- robot wrangler: resets robot starting locations, sets up obstacles, and performs any needed measurements

- documentarian: reads and organizes the Challenge Cards, records results, and takes photos or videos of robots

When students work together while coding, they're able to help each other identify mistakes and develop creative solutions!

Troubleshooting

You and your students are bound to run into some complications when using new technology. Help students help themselves by reviewing a few troubleshooting strategies in advance:

If your program is not running correctly. . .

- Make sure Dash and/or Dot are turned on.
- Make sure Dash and/or Dot are connected to the app by tapping the icon at the top right of the screen.
- Check the name of your robot. Make sure it's the same as the name of the robot connected to your app.
- Make sure your blocks are connected to the **When Start** block.
- Try restarting the app.

If Dash and/or Dot are disconnecting. . .

- Turn off the robots and turn them on again. Then reconnect the robots to the app by tapping the icon at the top right of the screen.
- Press play and then press stop to make the robots reset.
- Try charging the robots.

Three, then me!

- First, ask for help from three of your classmates. If you still need help, then ask the teacher

Problem Solving and Debugging

Sometimes students can get stuck on a particular challenge or problem. They may have an error or "bug" in their code. They may also have only partially solved the problem or misunderstood the challenge.

To provide challenge-specific hints, you can refer to the **Challenge Card Solutions** section of this guide. We also recommend that you review a few debugging strategies in advance to help students get unstuck on their own:

Break Down the Challenge:

- What do you need for the challenge? Which robots? Any other accessories or materials?
- What are Dash or Dot supposed to do?
- Have you solved similar challenges to this one?
- Focus on one step at a time.

Plan Your Solution

- Draw a picture or make a list of what you want Dash or Dot to do.
- What blocks will you need to complete the challenge?
- Are there any hints on the card that can help?
- Use tape to mark Dash's starting point.
- If there are obstacles in the challenge, use tape to mark each obstacle's location in case they get moved.

Test Your Code

- Does your code complete the challenge?

- If not, play your code again. Watch as the program goes through each block. Do you notice any mistakes?

- Are your blocks in the correct order?

- Do you need to add more blocks? Do you need to remove any blocks?

- Are your blocks telling Dash to do something when you actually want Dot to do something?

- Do your events match the instructions on the card?

- Are you starting Dash at the same position each time you run your program?

- Pretend to be Dash or Dot. Act out each block in your code and look for mistakes.

Improve Your Work

- Ask another student or group to check your program.

- Is there an easier way to complete the challenge? Can you use fewer blocks?

- How can you improve your program? Could you add more lights, sounds, or other customizations?

NOTE: You can find **Troubleshooting** and **Problem Solving & Debugging Handouts** in the **Appendix** of this guide.

23

Challenge Card Solutions

An Introduction

In this guide, we have provided a solution page for each of our 72 **Challenge Cards**. Each solution page provides the following information:

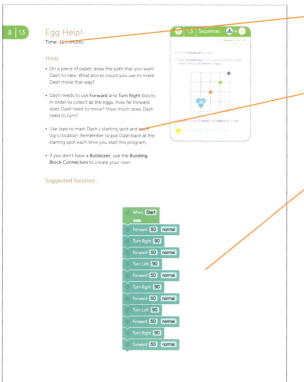

Estimated Time
Suggests the amount of time each challenge is estimated to take.

Hints
Includes 2-3 questions/hints that can be used to guide students toward a possible solution.

Suggested Solutions
Provides a possible solution to the challenge

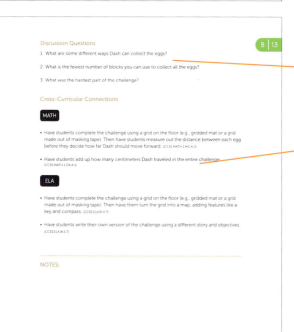

Discussion Questions
Includes 2-3 questions to wrap up the challenge after it's completed.

Cross-Curricular Connections
Provides ELA and Math Extension ideas that can be incorporated into the challenge.

A | 1.1 Ready, Set, Go!

Time: 5 minutes

Hints

- The **light** blocks are **dark blue**. You can find a **light** block by going to the **Lights** menu and selecting an **All Lights** block. Then tap on the block to select a color.

- The **animation** block is a different color. Go to the Animations menu and select a Race block.

Suggested Solution:

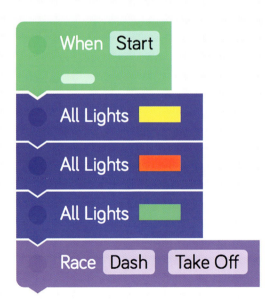

Discussion Questions

1. How could you add to the code? What other **lights** or **animations** would you like to add?

2. How do the blocks tell Dash what to do?

Cross-Curricular Connections

- Have students count how many **light** blocks and **animation** blocks were used. Then have them add the two types of blocks to determine the total number of **light** and **animation** blocks used. (CCSS.MATH.K.MD.B.3)

- Have students draw a series of pictures to illustrate Dash's program (e.g., yellow lights, red lights, green lights, Dash racing). (CCSS.ELA.W.K.3)

NOTES:

A | 1.2 Ready, Set, Dance!

Time: 10 minutes

Hints

- The **light** blocks are **dark blue**. You can find a **light** block by going to the **Lights** menu and selecting an **All Lights** block. Then tap on the block to select a color.

- The **animations** block is a different color. Go to the **Animations** menu and select a **dance** block.

Suggested Solution:

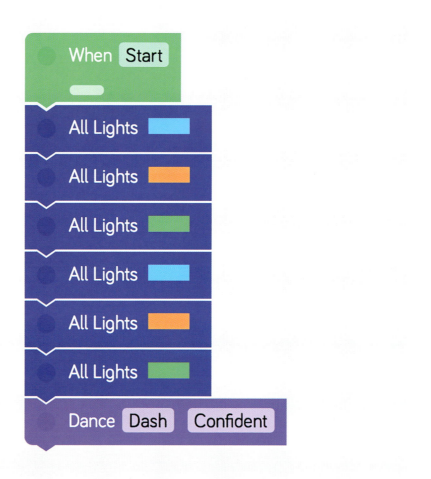

27

Discussion Questions

1. How can you make a new light pattern with this program?

2. How can you make a longer light pattern?

Cross-Curricular Connections

- Have students count how many blue **All Lights** blocks, orange **All Lights** blocks, and green **All Lights** blocks were used. Then have them add the **blue**, **orange**, and **green** blocks to determine the total number of blocks used. (CCSS.MATH.K.MD.B.3)

- Have students write the first letter of each color they used in the program (e.g., blue, orange, blue = B, O, B). Then, have students plan and try out a different color pattern by writing the first letter of each color and then using the corresponding blocks in the program. (CCSS.ELA.RF.K.2)

NOTES:

A | 1.3 Ready, Set, Rainbow!

Time: 10 minutes

Hints

- The **light** blocks are **dark blue**. You can find a **light** block by going to the **Lights** menu and selecting an **All Lights** block. Then tap on the block to select a color.

- You can choose any **animation**. Which one works best with the rainbow?

Suggested Solution:

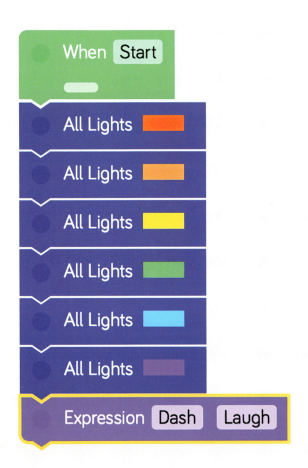

29

Discussion Questions

1. How could you make Dash show the **rainbow** twice?

2. How could you add **sound** blocks to the middle of the code? Which blocks would you want to use?

Cross-Curricular Connections

- Have students count how many **light** blocks, **sound** blocks, and **animation** blocks were used. Have them add the **start**, **light**, **sound**, and **animation** blocks to determine the total number of blocks used. (CCSS.MATH.K.MD.B.3)

- Have students draw a series of pictures to illustrate Dash's program (e.g., red lights, orange lights, Dash laughing, Dash making a funny sound, etc). (CCSS.ELA.W.K.3)

NOTES:

A | 2.1 Smile, Dot!

Time: 10 minutes

Hints

- You can find the **Eye Pattern** block in the **Light** menu.

- You can turn off all of Dot's **eye lights** by using the **Eye Pattern** block. Tap the **Eye Pattern** block and touch each light to turn it off.

- How can you program Dot to make a **sound**? Choose the **Say** block from the **Sound** menu. Tap the block and then tap **Dot** at the top of the menu to see all of Dot's sounds.

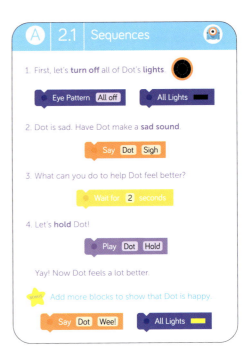

Suggested Solution:

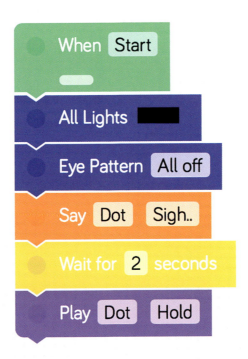

Discussion Questions

1. What **sound** blocks can you use to show that Dot is happy?

2. What **light** or **animation** blocks could you use to show that Dot is happy? Could you also use a different **Eye Pattern** block or different **colors**?

Cross-Curricular Connections

- Have students count aloud as they turn off each eye light. (CCSS.MATH.K.CC.A.3)

- Discuss why Dot might be sad and why Dot feels happy after being held. Then have students draw or write about what makes them feel sad and happy. (CCSS.ELA.W.K.8)

NOTES:

A | 2.2 Dot Count Down

Time: 10 minutes

Hints

- You can change Dot's eye lights by using the **Eye Pattern** block. Tap the **Eye Pattern** block and touch each light to turn it on or off.

- How can you program Dot to make a **sound**? Choose the **Say** block from the **Sound** menu. Tap the block and then tap **Dot** at the top of the menu to see all of Dot's sounds.

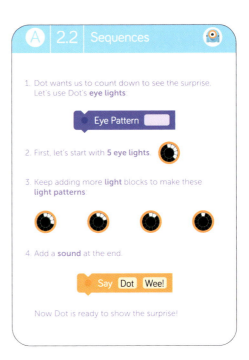

Suggested Solution:

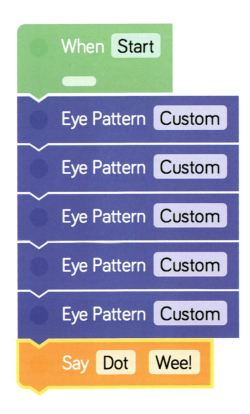

33

Discussion Questions

1. What do you think Dot's surprise will be?

2. How can you change the code to count down from 12 instead of 5?

Cross-Curricular Connections

- Have students count down out loud as each of Dot's lights turn out (e.g., "5, 4, 3, 2, 1!").
  (CCSS.MATH.K.CC.A.3)

- Have students write about and/or draw a picture illustrating what they think Dot's surprise might be. (CCSS.ELA.W.K.8)

NOTES:

A | 2.3 Dot's Surprise!

Time: 10 minutes

Hints

- You can change Dot's **eye lights** by using the **Eye Pattern** block. Tap the **Eye Pattern** block and touch each light to turn it on or off.

- How can you program Dot to do a **dance**? Choose the **Dance** block from the **Animation** menu. Tap the block and then tap **Dot** at the top to see all of Dot's animations.

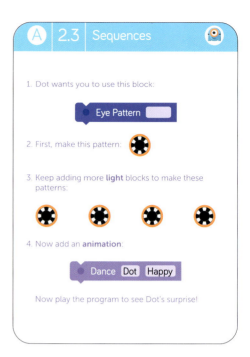

Suggested Solution:

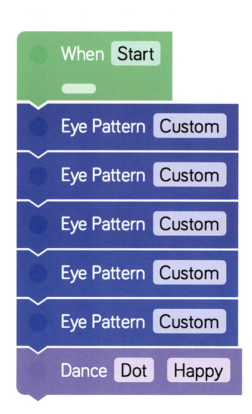

35

Discussion Questions

1. What did you notice about Dot's surprise? Did Dot's eye lights make a pattern? What kind of pattern did Dot's eyes make?

2. How could you add to Dot's surprise? Could you add more lights? More sounds?

Cross-Curricular Connections

- Have students count how many eye lights were used in each custom eye pattern (e.g., 6). (CCSS.MATH.K.CC.A.3)

- Have students create a surprise for Dot. Have them write and draw pictures to illustrate the surprise. What sounds and lights could they use? (CCSS.ELA.W.K.3)

NOTES:

A | 2.4

Dash Saves the Day!

Time: 15 minutes

Hints

- Try one **Forward** block and see how far Dash goes. How many more blocks do you think you'll need to help Dash get to the toy?

- Make sure Dash is facing the toy and that Dash's wheels are straight before you press play.

Suggested Solution:

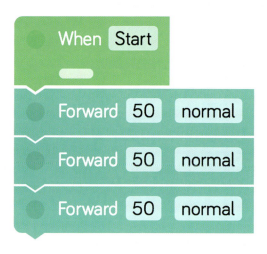

37

Discussion Questions

1. How many blocks did it take for Dash to get to the toy?

2. Try using fewer blocks. Tap on the Forward block to change how far Dash moves forward.

3. What sounds or lights can you have Dash play after the toy is saved?

Cross-Curricular Connections

- Have students explore how the challenge can be solved in different ways (e.g., with one **Forward** block versus multiple **Forward** blocks). (CCSS.MATH.K.MD.A.2)

- Have students write about or draw a picture showing why the monster wants to eat Dash's toy. (CCSS.ELA.W.K.3)

NOTES:

A | 2.5 Dash the Guard

Time: 20 minutes

Hints

- Use tape to mark Dash's starting spot and the toy's location. Remember to put Dash back at the starting spot each time you start the program.

- How many sides are in a square? That's how many **Forward** blocks you need.

- When do you need Dash to **turn right**? How many turns do you think Dash needs to make?

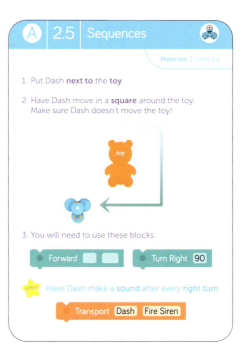

Suggested Solution:

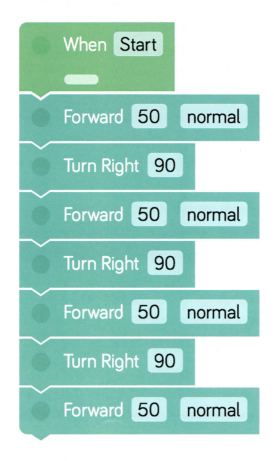

Discussion Questions

1. What blocks do you need to make Dash guard the toy with **left turns**?

2. What kinds of sounds should Dash make after each turn? What sound would you make if you were the toy guard?

Cross-Curricular Connections

- Have students count how many **Forward** and **Right Turn** blocks were used in the program. Then have them calculate the total number of blocks used. (CCSS.MATH.K.MD.B.3)

- Have students write about or draw a picture showing how Dash guarded the toy. Then have them write about or draw a picture showing other ways Dash could guard the toy. (CCSSELA.W.K.3)

NOTES:

A | 2.6 Dash Guards Again!

Time: 20 minutes

Hints

- Use tape to mark Dash's starting spot and the toy's location. Remember to put Dash back at the starting spot each time you start the program.

- Two sides of a rectangle are longer than the other two. Dash will need to move forward farther for those sides.

- When do you need Dash to **turn right**? How many turns do you think Dash needs to make?

Suggested Solution:

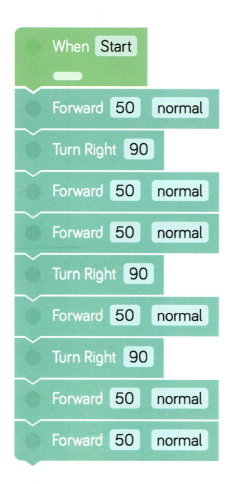

Discussion Questions

1. How can you change the program to make Dash guard the toys using a different number of blocks or different types of blocks (e.g., **Turn Left** blocks instead of **Turn Right** blocks)?

2. What kinds of sounds and lights should Dash make after each turn? What sounds would you make if you were the toy guard?

Cross-Curricular Connections

- Have students talk about the sides of the rectangle path made by Dash. Which sides have the same length? How many corners are there? (CCSS.MATH.K.G.B.4)

- Have students write about or draw a picture showing how Dash guarded the toys. Then have them write about or draw a picture showing other ways Dash could guard the toys.
  (CCSS.ELA.W.K.3)

NOTES:

A | 3.1 The Forever Light Show

Time: 15 minutes

Hints

- The **Repeat Forever** block is yellow. Find the block in the yellow **Control** menu.

- Make sure you put the **light** blocks **inside** the **Repeat Forever** block.

Suggested Solution:

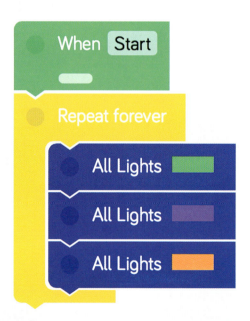

43

Discussion Questions

1. What kinds of sounds and animations would you like to add to Dot's Forever Light Show?

2. Remember Dash's light shows in Challenge Cards A 1.1 and A 1.2? How can we make Dash's light shows go on forever?

Cross-Curricular Connections

- Have students count how many light blocks were used. Then have them count the total number of blocks used. (CCSS.MATH.K.MD.B.3)

- Have students draw a series of pictures to illustrate Dot's program (e.g., green light, purple light, orange light). Have them use arrows to show the loop in the program.
(CCSS.ELA.W.K.3)

NOTES:

A | 3.2 Dance, Dash, Dance!

Time: 15 minutes

Hints

- The **Repeat Forever** block is yellow. Find the block in the yellow **Control** menu.

- You get to choose how many blocks to put inside the **Repeat Forever** block. Make sure you use at least one **drive** block, one **light** block, and one **sound** block.

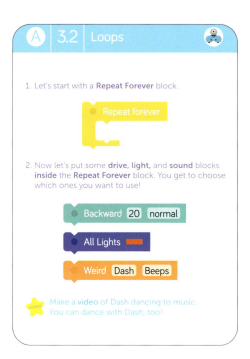

Suggested Solution:

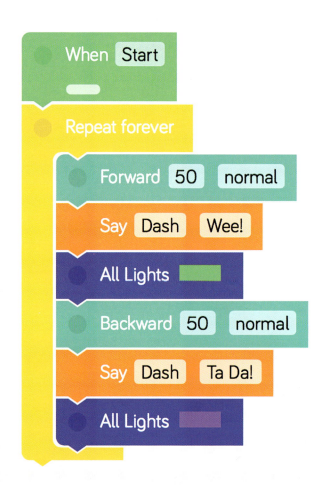

Discussion Questions

1. What kind of music do you want to use for Dash's dance? How can we program Dash's dance to go with the music?

2. Why do you think we used a loop to create Dash's dance?

Cross-Curricular Connections

- Have students count how many **drive**, **light**, and **sound** blocks were used. Then have them count the total number of blocks used. (CCSS.MATH.K.MD.B.3)

- Have students create a song for Dash's dance. Then have them record the song and play it while Dash dances. (CCSS.ELA.W.K.6)

NOTES:

A | 3.3 Dash Guards a Lot!

Time: 20 minutes

Hints

- The **Repeat Forever** block is yellow. Find the block in the yellow **Control** menu.

- Make sure you put the blocks you choose **inside** the **Repeat** block.

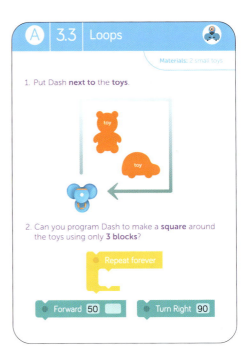

Suggested Solution:

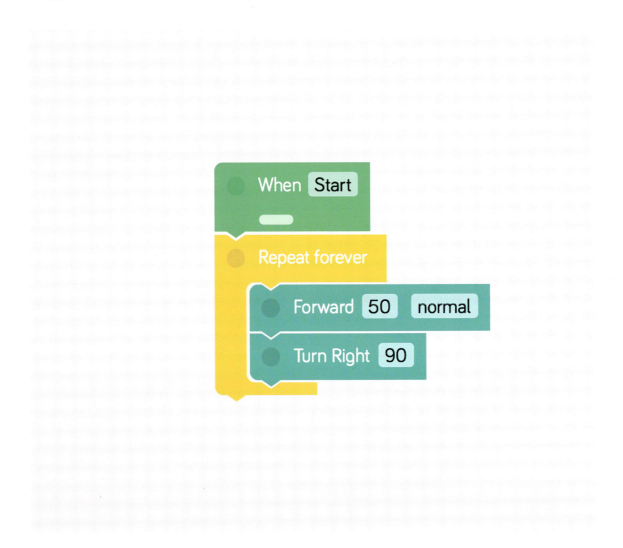

47

Discussion Questions

1. What kinds of sounds should Dash make after each turn? What sounds would you make if you were the guard?

2. How does the loop help Dash guard the toys in a better way?

Cross-Curricular Connections

- Have students write a tally mark each time Dash makes a square. Have them call out when Dash has made 5 squares and stop the program. Repeat the activity using different numbers of squares. (CCSS.MATH.K.MD.B.3)

- Have students draw pictures showing how many times Dash guarded the toys. This could be a series of pictures (1 for each time Dash makes the square) or a diagram to show the loops using arrows. (CCSS.ELA.W.K.3)

NOTES:

B | 1.1 Dash the Collector

Time: 10 minutes

Hints

- If you don't have a **Bulldozer**, use the **Building Block Connectors** to create your own.

- Tap the **Forward** block and drag the **arrow up** or **down** to change how far Dash moves.

- You can record your own sound by tapping on the **My Sounds** block. Then press **Record a New Sound**, choose a number slot, and tap the microphone to record your sound.

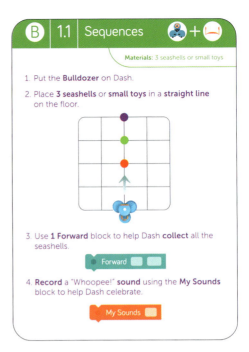

Suggested Solution:

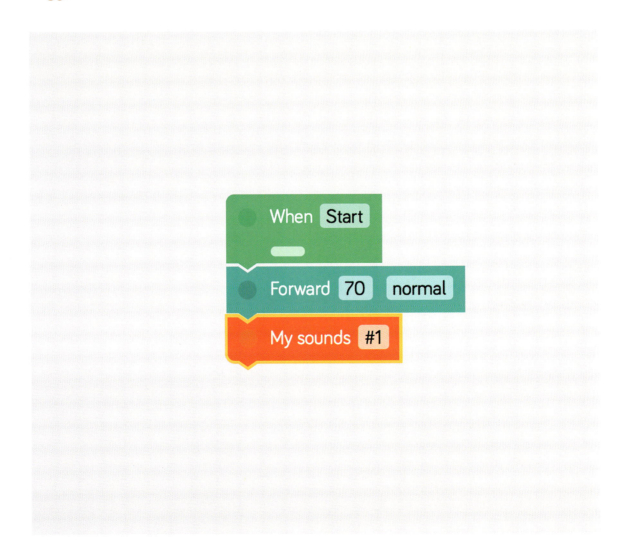

49

Discussion Questions

1. How would you need to change the program if there were **5 seashells** instead of 3?

2. What if you wanted Dash to make a sound after each seashell was collected? What would you need to add to the program? What would you need to change?

Cross-Curricular Connections

MATH

- Have students measure out the distance between each seashell before they decide how far Dash should move forward. (CCSS.MATH.MD.A.2)

ELA

- Have students complete the challenge using a grid on the floor (e.g., gridded mat or a grid made out of masking tape). Then have them turn the grid into a map, adding features like a key and compass. (CCSS.ELA.RI.K.7)

- Have students write their own version of the challenge using a different story and objectives. (CCSS.ELA.W.1.7)

NOTES:

B | 1.2 It's Candy Time!

Time: 15 minutes

Hints

- If you don't have a **Bulldozer**, use the **Building Block Connectors** to create your own.

- Use your finger to trace the path that you want Dash to take. What's the first block you'll need to get Dash started on the path? Is it a **Forward** block or a **Turn Right** block?

- You can **record** your own sound by tapping on the **My Sounds** block. Then press **Record a New Sound**, choose a number slot, and tap the microphone to record your sound.

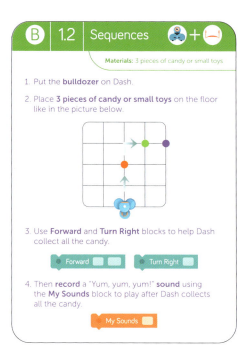

Suggested Solution:

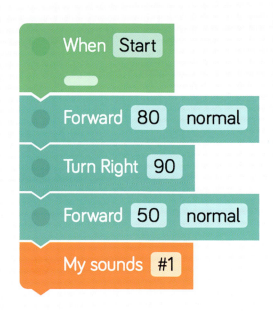

Discussion Questions

1. How would you need to change the program if Dash were facing a different direction at the start of the path?

2. What if you wanted Dash to make a sound after each piece of candy was collected? What would you need to add to the program? What would you need to change?

Cross-Curricular Connections

- Have students measure out the distance between each piece of candy before they decide how far Dash should move forward. (CCSS.MATH.MD.A.2)

- Have students complete the challenge using a grid on the floor (e.g., gridded mat or a grid made out of masking tape). Then have them turn the grid into a map, adding features like a key and compass. (CCSS.ELA.RI.K.7)

- Have students write their own version of the challenge using a different story and objectives. (CCSS.ELA.W.1.7)

NOTES:

Egg Help!

Time: 15 minutes

Hints

- On a piece of paper, draw the path that you want Dash to take. What blocks could you use to make Dash move that way?

- Dash needs to use **Forward** and **Turn Right** blocks. In order to collect all the eggs, how far forward does Dash need to move? How much does Dash need to turn?

- Use tape to mark Dash's starting spot and each toy's location. Remember to put Dash back at the starting spot each time you start the program.

- If you don't have a **Bulldozer**, use the **Building Block Connectors** to create your own.

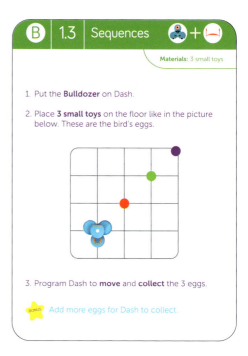

Suggested Solution:

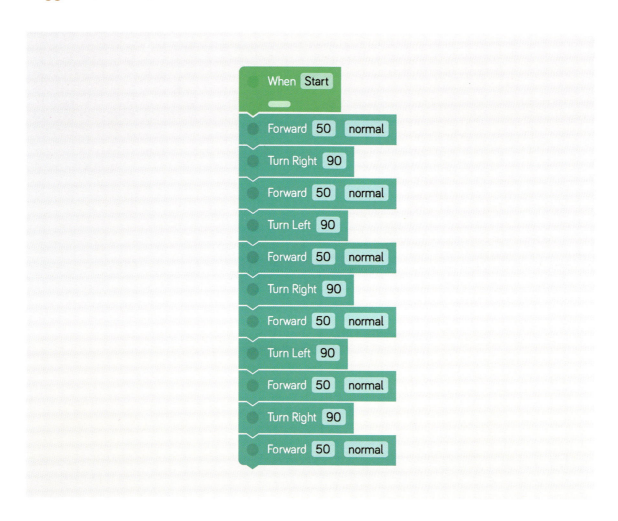

Discussion Questions

1. What are some different ways Dash can collect the eggs?

2. What is the fewest number of blocks you can use to collect all the eggs?

3. What was the hardest part of the challenge?

Cross-Curricular Connections

MATH

- Have students complete the challenge using a grid on the floor (e.g., gridded mat or a grid made out of masking tape). Then have students measure out the distance between each egg before they decide how far Dash should move forward. (CCSS.MATH.1.MD.A.2)

- Have students add up how many centimeters Dash traveled in the entire challenge. (CCSS.MATH.1.OA.A.1)

ELA

- Have students complete the challenge using a grid on the floor (e.g., gridded mat or a grid made out of masking tape). Then have them turn the grid into a map, adding features like a key and compass. (CCSS.ELA.RI.K.7)

- Have students write their own version of the challenge using a different story and objectives. (CCSS.ELA.W.1.7)

NOTES:

Petting Zoo

Time: 5-10 minutes

Hints

- Look for the **Repeat Forever** and **Wait For** blocks in the **Control** menu.

- The **Random** selection is the very last option in the **Animal** sound block menu. Don't forget to select Dot.

- Place the **Animal** sound and **Wait For** blocks inside the **Repeat Forever** block.

Suggested Solution:

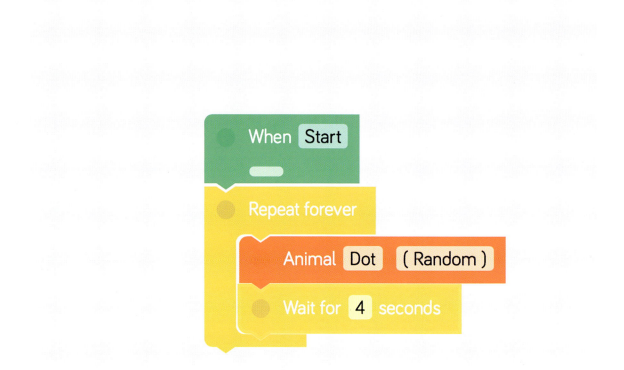

Discussion Questions

1. If you change the order of the blocks, are you still able to guess what animal Dot is petting?

2. What if you only wanted to play the game 3 times? How could you change the code to make this happen?

Cross-Curricular Connections

- Have students count how many animals Dot has heard. (CCSS.MATH.K.CC.B.4)

- Have students listen to Dot. For every sound Dot makes, have students say or write an adjective describing that animal. Have students share the adjectives with a partner and have partners guess the animal the adjectives are describing. (CCSS.ELA.L.1.1.F)

- Isolate the initial and final phoneme of each animal's name (e.g., for alligator, a is the initial phoneme and r is the final phoneme). Encourage students to repeat each phoneme. (CCSS.ELA.W.1.7)

NOTES:

B | 2.2 Quick, Hide!

Time: 10-15 minutes

Hints

- To turn off all of Dot's ear lights, choose the color black.

- To turn off all of Dot's eye lights, tap on each light around the eye.

- Place all of the blocks inside the **Repeat Forever** block. Only the blocks inside the **Repeat Forever** block will be repeated.

Suggested Solution:

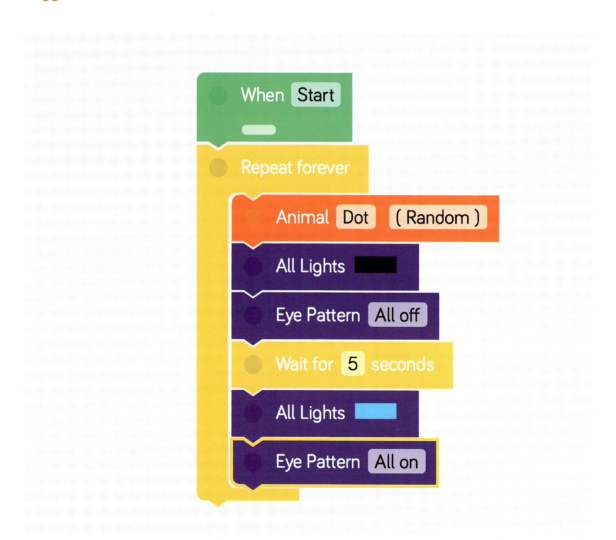

57

Discussion Questions

1. Look in the **Animation** menu. Is there an animation you could add to the loop that would make the story even more interesting? (Hint: Look under **Play**.) Where in the loop would you add this block?

2. What could you change so that Dot will only hide a certain number of times? (Hint: Choose a different **Repeat** block.)

Cross-Curricular Connections

- Have students use a missing variable and sum to find the total number of loops that Dot went through in the program. (CCSS.MATH.1.OA.B.4)

- Have students describe the places Dot could hide in the classroom. Students must use correct positional words (e.g., over, under, next to, to the right) to describe the locations. (CCSS.MATH.K.G.A.1)

- Have students get into groups. Assign each group one or two of the animals Dot encounters at the zoo. Have groups research, write, and present facts about the animals to the class. (CCSS.ELA.W.1.2)

NOTES:

B | 2.3 You Are Getting Sleepy...

Time: 20-25 minutes

Hints

- Change the number in the **Repeat** block to **5**.

- To change the **Eye Pattern** block, tap on each light to turn it on or off.

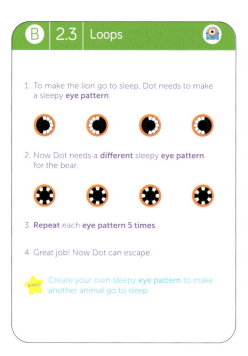

Suggested Solution:

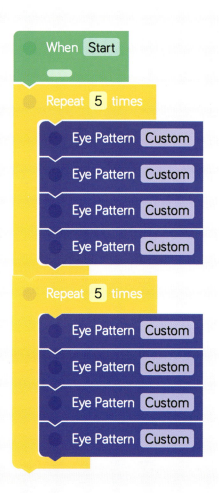

59

Discussion Questions

1. Could we use the **Repeat Forever** or **Repeat Until** block for this challenge? Why or why not?

2. Could you add **ear lights** or **sounds** to the loop?

Cross-Curricular Connections

- Have students count the lit and unlit lights in each of Dot's **Eye Patterns**. (CCSS.MATH.K.CC.B.4.A)

- Have students write a narrative that tells how the animals escaped. (CCSS.ELA-W.1.3)

NOTES:

B | 2.4 Littered Lake

Time: 15-20 minutes

Hints

- The **Repeat** block is in the **Control** menu.

- To change the number of centimeters Dash moves forward, tap on the **Forward** block and move the arrow slider up and down.

- If you don't have a **Bulldozer**, use the **Building Block Connectors** to create your own.

Suggested Solution:

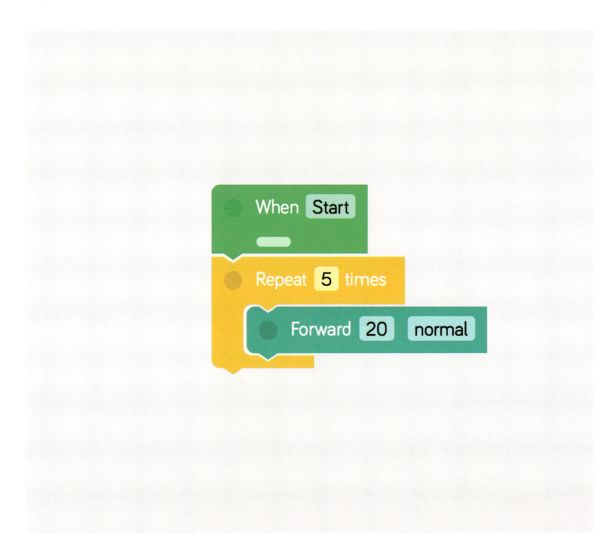

Discussion Questions

1. What happens if you repeat the program **3 times** instead of 5? What happens if you repeat **8 times**?

2. Why do you have to place Dash in front of all the trash? What would happen if you placed Dash to the left or right of the line of trash and run the program?

Cross-Curricular Connections

- Have students write the equation they programmed (i.e., 20+20+20+20+20=100).
  (CCSS.MATH.1.NBT.B.2.C)

- Have students write a different equation and use the **Repeat** block to demonstrate it.
  (CCSS.MATH..1.OA.A.1)

- Have students write a poem or song reminding people why it's important to keep our rivers and lakes clean. (CCSS.ELA.W.1.7)

- Have students make a poster advertising a campaign to stop littering. (CCSS.ELA.W.1.8)

NOTES:

B 2.5 Recycling Rush

Time: 20-25 minutes

Hints

- Make sure the **Drive** and **Turn** blocks are **inside** the **Repeat** block.

- To make this program run smoothly, space the cups evenly. Use a ruler and put the cups 20 centimeters apart.

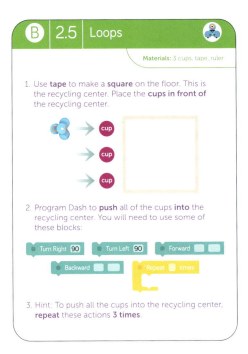

Suggested Solution:

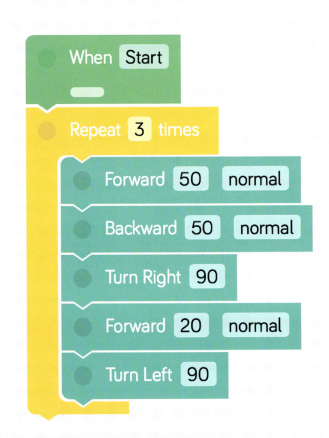

Discussion Questions

1. Do the cups have to be the same distance apart in order for the program to work? Why or why not?

2. What happens if you repeat the loop **5 times**?

Cross-Curricular Connections

- Guide the class in writing an equation to determine how many centimeters Dash traveled during this challenge. Work with the students to simplify the equation to make it easier to read. (i.e., 50+50+20+50+50+20+50+50+20=360). (CCSS.MATH.1.NBT.C.4, CCSS.MATH.2.NBT.B.5)

- Have students measure the perimeter and/or area of the Recycling Center. (CCSS.MATH.3.MD.D.8)

- Have students research and write about the reasons recycling is important. (CCSS.ELA-LITERACY.W.1.7)

- Have students use old magazines and newspapers to create a collage of items that can be recycled. Ask students to present their work to the class. (CCSS.ELA.SL.1.5)

NOTES:

B | 2.6 Dash's Trash

Time: 40-45 minutes

Hints

- Write a program that takes Dash up to the top of the lake and back down to the bottom. **Repeat** this block of code several times to make Dash clean up the entire lake.

- Dash has to **Turn** and **Drive Forward 10** cm at the end of every line.

Suggested Solution:

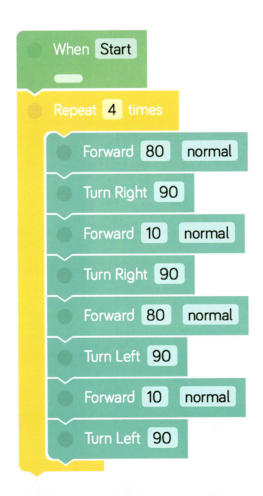

Discussion Questions

1. How many times do you need Dash to repeat this block of code in order for Dash to clean up the entire lake? How can you figure this out?

2. If you change Dash's starting location or direction, can you still use the same program? Why or why not?

3. What would happen if you programmed Dash to do a **180 degree turn** at the opposite side of the lake instead of **turning 90 degrees** and then **driving forward 10 cm**?

Cross-Curricular Connections

- Have students stand up. Run the program and every time Dash turns 90 degrees, encourage the students to turn 90 degrees. Have students keep track of the number of complete circles they make. Students could also total the number of degrees they traveled.
  (CCSS.MATH.4.MD.C.5.A)

- Have students figure out the total number of centimeters Dash traveled during this challenge. (CCSS.MATH.3.OA.D.8)

- Have students research and discuss and/or write why it is important to keep our lakes and rivers clean. (CCSS.ELA-SL.3.1, CCSS.ELA-SL.3.4, CCSS.ELA-W.3.2)

- Have students write an opinion piece about why keeping our lakes and rivers clean is important. (CCSS.ELA-W.3.1)

NOTES:

On Your Mark!

Time: 10 minutes

Hints

- Dash makes all kinds of sounds. Look in the **Transport** sound block for the **Car Engine** sound.

- Find the **Wait For** block in the **Control** menu.

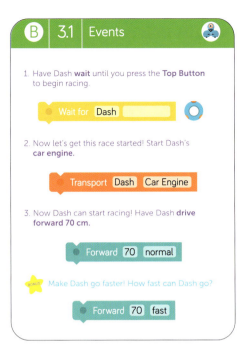

Suggested Solution:

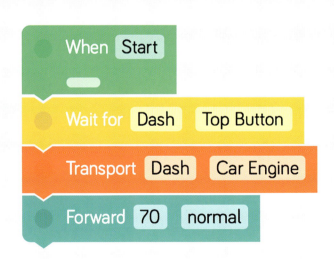

Discussion Questions

1. How did you change Dash's speed?

2. Were you able to change the way you told Dash to start the race? How?

Cross-Curricular Connections

- Have students estimate how far 70 centimeters is before they begin the challenge. Have students mark their estimates on the floor with tape. Discuss their results. (CCSS.MATH.1.NBT.C.4,CCSS.MATH.2.NBT.B.5)

- Have students measure 70 centimeters with a variety of non-standard units (e.g., paperclips, pencils) and count how many Dash traveled. (CCSS.MATH.1.MD.A.2)

- Have students program Dash to move 10 centimeters at a time. Have them calculate how many times they have to repeat 10 centimeters before Dash gets to 70 centimeters? (CCSS.MATH.1.MD.A.2)

- Place sight words you've pre-written on cards on the ground. Each time Dash rolls over a word, have the students read it. (Hint: Change the speed to slow.) (CCSS.ELA.RF.K.3.C)

- Place letters you've pre-written on cards on the ground. The letters should form words (or onset and rimes). As Dash rolls over each letter or letter combination, have students produce the associated phonemes to read the word. (CCSS.ELA.RF.1.3)

- Use Dash as a model for proper sentence construction. The starting line can represent a capital letter and the finish line can represent the period (or other ending punctuation). (CCSS.ELA.RF.1.3)

NOTES:

B | 3.2 Get Set!

Time: 15 minutes

Hints

- Use the cue **Hear Voice** in the **Wait For** block to tell Dash to listen to your voice.

- You can record your own sound by tapping on the **My Sounds block**. Then press **Record a New Sound**, choose a number slot, and tap the microphone to record your sound.

Suggested Solution:

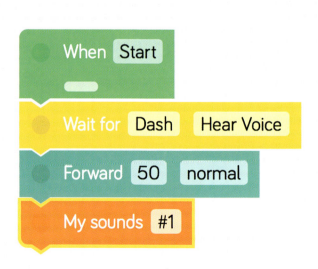

Discussion Questions

1. How could you get Dash across the finish line if the finish line were further than 100 centimeters away?

2. Could you use the same blocks in a different order and have Dash still finish the race? What happens if you change the block order?

Cross-Curricular Connections

- Have students solve a variety of math problems that use addends that are multiples of 10 (Dash can only travel in increments of 10 centimeters). Have them use a different **drive** block to represent each numeral. Use Dash to demonstrate the problem. (CCSS.MATH.1.NBT.C.6)

- Use Dash to solve for a missing addend. (CCSS.MATH.1.OA.B.4)

- Write a program using 2 or more **drive** blocks. Have them represent the **drive** blocks as a mathematical equation. (CCSS.MATH.1.NBT.C.6)

ELA

- Have students record the beginning, middle, and end of a story using 3 different **sound** blocks. Have Dash tell the beginning of the story at the starting line. Then, program Dash to stop in the middle of the race course and tell the middle of the story. Finally, have Dash tell the end of the story after crossing the finish line. (CCSS.ELA.RL.1.2)

- Place pre-written sentence strips containing frequently-used phrases or sentences on the floor. Place the beginning of the strip at the starting line. Set Dash's speed at very slow. As Dash rolls by each word, have students read the phrases or sentences. Increase Dash's speed as the students' fluency becomes better. (CCSS.ELA.RF.1.4.B)

NOTES:

Go, Go, Go!

Time: 20 minutes

Hints

- Place all the **drive** blocks needed to make Dash complete the race course in a **Repeat** block. When we use **Repeat** blocks, it makes our code easier to read and change.

- Each corner of a square or rectangle is a 90-degree angle. All the turns Dash makes should be 90 degrees.

- Make sure you wave the flag low enough so that Dash's sensors can "see" it.

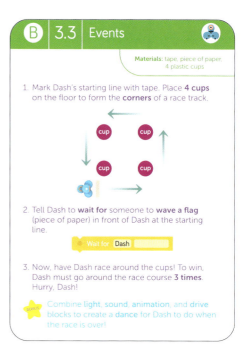

Suggested Solution:

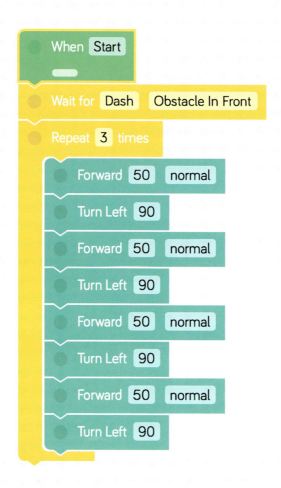

Discussion Questions

1. Could you still get Dash to finish the race if you wrote the code in a different way than you just did?

2. Would the program need to change if you placed the cups in a diamond shape instead of a square shape? Why or why not?

Cross-Curricular Connections

- Mark 10-centimeter squares on the floor using tape or a gridded mat. Have students determine the perimeter and/or area of Dash's race track. Use addition and multiplication formulas to find an answer. Move the cups. How does it affect the totals?
  (CCSS.MATH.3.MD.C.5, CCSS.MATH.3.MD.D.8)

- Create different-shaped race courses with the cups (e.g., rectangle, triangle). Have students use protractors to measure the angles needed to finish the race. (CCSS.MATH.4.MD.C.6)

- Have students use the race track to tell a simple story. Tell them that each corner of the race track represents the beginning, middle, and end of the story. When Dash rounds each corner, students should record and program Dash to tell that part of the story. (CCSS.ELA.W.1.3)

NOTES:

C | 1.1 No Homework!

Time: 20 minutes

Hints

- What direction does Dash need to turn? On the **turn** blocks, point the Dash in your app in the direction you want your robot to go.

- To make Dash look a different direction, choose the **Look** block and move the arrow around to the **right**, **left**, or **center** (to make Dash look forward).

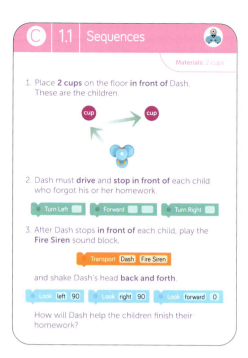

Suggested Solution:

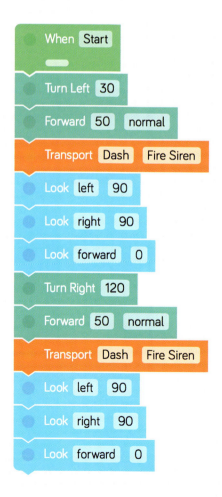

73

Discussion Questions

1. What blocks could you add to make Dash's lights flash **3 times** once the children are back in school?

2. Can all of your **turn** blocks use the same number in this challenge? Why or why not?

Cross-Curricular Connections

- Have students use protractors to measure the angles Dash needs to use to get to the children. (CCSS.MATH.4.MD.C.)

- Have students write a different story to go with the code they've just written. Who does Dash need to catch and why? Have students decorate their cups to help tell their story. (CCSS.ELA.W.2.3)

NOTES:

C | 1.2 Come Back!

Time: 30-35 minutes

Hints

- To get Dash to push the children into the school, first program Dash to move behind the cups and then program Dash to drive **Forward**.

- Every time you test your program, make sure you start Dash from the same location. Put tape on the floor under each cup so they also start in the same position.

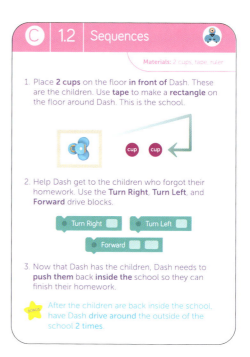

Suggested Solution:

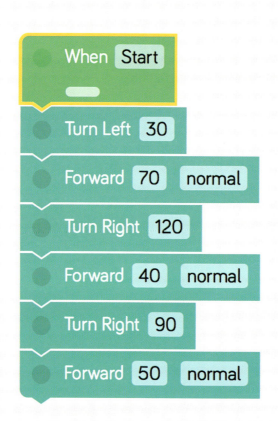

75

Discussion Questions

1. What blocks could you add to make Dash's lights flash **3 times** once the children are back in school?

2. Can all of your **turn** blocks use the same number in this challenge? Why or why not?

Cross-Curricular Connections

- Have students use a protractor to measure and find the best path for Dash. Have them draw their predictions (angles) on paper, measure them, and use them to predict Dash's path. (CCSS.MATH.4.MD.C)

- Have students write a story about why the children might have forgotten their homework at school (e.g., the dog ate it). Encourage humorous responses. (CCSS.ELA.RF.1.2.B)

- Have students think of a fun homework assignment for the "children" in the challenge that practices spelling (students may use the spelling list from the current week). The homework must be so much fun that the children would never forget it at school. (CCSS.ELA.L.1.2.D)

NOTES:

C | 1.3

Wait!

Time: 30-35 minutes

Hints

- Make sure that Dash and Dot are both turned on and connected to the **Blockly** app.

- Dash finds Dot best when Dot's eye is at the same level as Dash's. If necessary, place **books** underneath Dot to increase Dot's height. Also, put Dot far enough away so that Dash can see Dot's eye.

- To help Dash make it through the cups, minor changes can make a big difference.

- Program Dash to get past one cup at a time. Don't try to program Dash through the entire course all at once.

Suggested Solution:

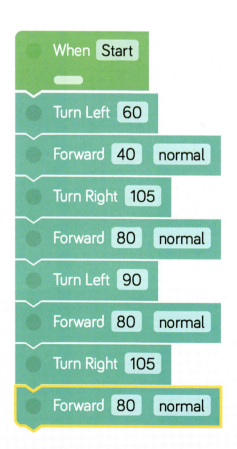

Discussion Questions

1. Could you write this program using a loop and get the same results? Why or why not?

2. Could Dash use an accessory to deliver Dot's homework? Which one? If you were to design your own accessory to deliver Dot's homework, what would it look like?

Cross-Curricular Connections

- Use each cup as an in/out box. Choose or have the students choose a rule (e.g., add 3 and a beginning digit). As Dash passes each cup, students must apply the rule to each subsequent number and call out the sum at the end. (CCSS.MATH.4.OA.C.5)

- Write temporal and linking phrases on top of each cup (e.g., First, Also, Next). As Dash rolls by each cup, students must say a sentence that begins each phrase.
(CCSS.ELA.W.3.3.C, CCSS.ELA.W.3.2.C)

NOTES:

C 2.1 Connect the Dots

Time: 15 minutes

Hints

- On a piece of paper, sketch out how you would like Dot's eye to look before you program.

- After you're done designing Dot's **eye patterns**, tap the arrow on the bottom to return to your code.

Suggested Solution:

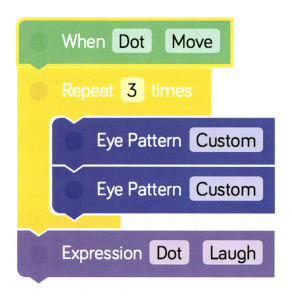

Discussion Questions

1. What different kinds of patterns can you make with Dot's eye?
2. What would it look like if you programmed the lights in Dot's eye to be all on then all off?

Cross-Curricular Connections

- Have students name all of the shapes they see on Dot. What different shapes can Dot's eye lights make? (CCSS.MATH.K.G.A.1)

- Have students use Dot's eye patterns to make their own addition and subtraction problems. (E.g., Light up 4 of Dot's eye lights. Then light up 5 of Dot's eye lights and calculate the total number of Dot's eye lights that were turned on.) (CCSS.MATH.1.OA.A.1)

- Have students write an opinion piece about why it makes Dot so happy to move. (CCSS.ELA.W.1.1)

NOTES:

C | 2.2   The Dot Show

Time: 15 minutes

Hints

- Use the cue **Shake** in the **When** block so Dot knows when to start the show.

- On a piece of paper, sketch out what you would like Dot's eye to look like.

- Use the cue **Hear Clap** in a separate **When** block so Dot knows when to perform a special surprise.

- Think about some things Dot might say or sounds that Dot might make for the special surprise.

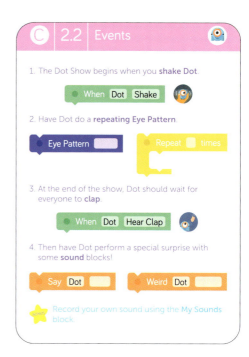

Suggested Solution:

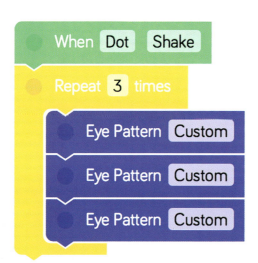

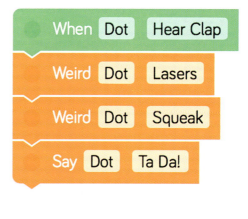

Discussion Questions

1. Explain how you could code Dot to respond to being tossed.

2. Describe what else Dot can do when moved.

Cross-Curricular Connections

- Have students customize a **sound** block to make Dot count by twos. (CCSS.MATH.1.OA.C.5)

- Have students describe the sounds they selected for Dot to make and why they chose those sounds. (CCSS.ELA.W.1.2)

- Have students draw a picture of Dot and add a speech bubble. In the speech bubble, have them write something Dot might say. (CCSS.ELA.W.K.2)

NOTES:

C 2.3 It's Your Turn!

Time: 20 minutes

Hints

- On a piece of paper, sketch out what you would like Dot's eye patterns to look like.

- Make sure you have at least **3 When** blocks for your program. Change each **When** block so that there is one for each orange button on Dot's head (i.e., **Button 1**, **Button 2**, **Button 3**).

Suggested Solution:

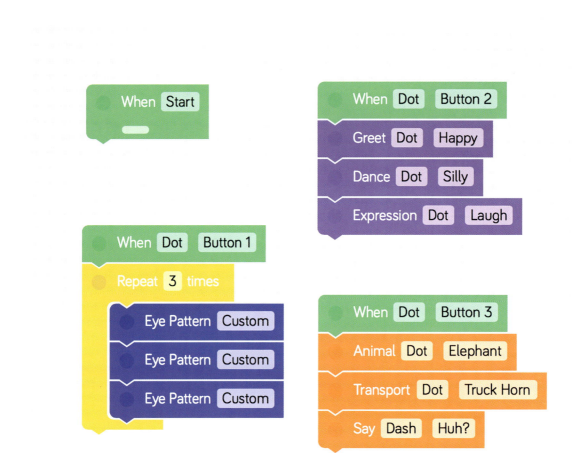

Discussion Questions

1. What are some other combinations you could try with the **When** blocks? Think about how many ways you can start a program with Dot.

2. How many **Repeat** blocks could be used in this program? How could repeat blocks help us improve the program?

Cross-Curricular Connections

- Have students draw a three-dimensional replica of Dot using their knowledge of geometric shapes. (CCSS.MATH.1.G.A.2)

- Have students write or draw a description of what Dot has done in their program. Then have them record a video of their program. (CCSS.ELA.W.1.6)

NOTES:

C | 2.4 Sleepy Time

Time: 10-15 minutes

Hints

- The **When** block is found in the **Start** menu. Tap on the block and tap on **Dot's** name to find Dot's actions.

- Find some silly sounds in the **Sound** menu.

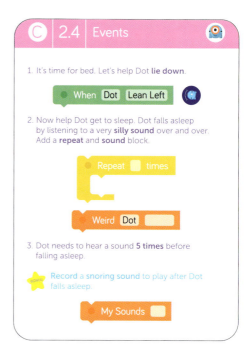

Suggested Solution:

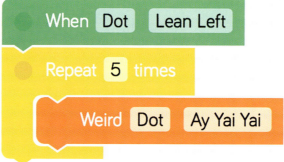

85

Discussion Questions

1. What other blocks could you use to help Dot go to sleep?

2. What if Dot were human? What types of sounds could you play to put Dot to bed?

Cross-Curricular Connections

- Have students run the program several times using a different sound each time. Use a timer to see which sound makes Dot fall asleep the fastest. Put the times in order from the slowest to the fastest. Find the average of the times. Find the difference between the length of each sound. (CCSS.MATH.4.MD.A.2)

- Using a timer, have students record the amount of time it takes for Dot to fall asleep for each sound. Then have them convert the time into a fraction (e.g. 3.25 seconds = 3 ¼). Put the fractions on a number line in the correct order. (CCSS.MATH.4.MD.B.4)

- Have students research strategies that help people sleep. Then have them write a how-to paragraph describing a successful bedtime routine for Dot. Make sure they use specific details. (CCSS.ELA.W.3.7, CCSS.ELA.W.3.2)

NOTES:

Wake Up!

Time: 10-15 minutes

Hints

- Find the **When** block in the **Start** menu.

- Dot's confused sound can be found in the **Sound** menu under **Say**.

- To turn all of Dot's lights off, tap on the **All Lights** block and choose black.

Suggested Solution:

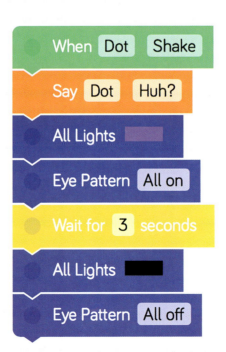

87

Discussion Questions

1. What other ways could you wake up Dot?

2. How could you write this program without using the **When** block and have the same outcome?

Cross-Curricular Connections

- Have students write the number of seconds Dot is asleep as an equation (e.g., 3+3+3+3). Create an array demonstrating the equation. Change the wait time and then repeat the activity. (CCSS.MATH.3.NBT.A.3, CCSS.MATH.2.OA.C.4)

- Have students write about the dream (or nightmare) Dot was having when they woke Dot up. (CCSS.ELA-.W.3.3)

NOTES:

C | 2.6

Lights Out!

Time: 10-15 minutes

Hints

- The **When** block is found in the **Start** menu. Tap on the block and tap on **Dot's** name to find Dot's actions.

- Find some silly sounds in the **Sound** menu.

Suggested Solution:

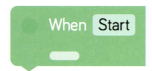

89

Discussion Questions

1. Could you change the program below each **When** block or does it have to be the same code in order to get the same result? Why or why not?

2. Did you have any problems running this program? If so, how could you fix them?

Cross-Curricular Connections

- Practice elapsed time. Tell the students what time Dot must wake up. What time does Dot need to go to bed in order to get ten hours of sleep? (CCSS.MATH.4.MD.A.2)

- Have students prepare a presentation about their favorite book. Ask them to include why Dot should or should not stay up reading the book they chose. (CCSS.ELA.W.3.2, CCSS.ELA.SL.3.4)

NOTES:

C | 3.1 Spaceship Spinout!

Time: 10 minutes

Hints

- To get Dash to turn in a circle, the **left** and **right wheel speeds** must be different. Tap on the **Set Wheel Speed** block and use the dials on the bottom to set the speed of the left and right wheels.

- To turn left, the right wheel needs to be faster than the left wheel in the **Set Wheel Speed** block. To turn right, the left wheel needs to be faster than the right wheel.

Suggested Solution:

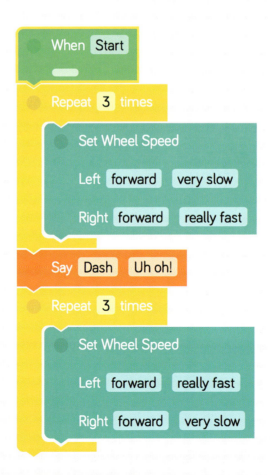

Discussion Questions

1. What would happen if the left and right wheels were going at the same speed? What would happen if one wheel were moving forward and one wheel were moving backward?

2. How could you change the program so that Dash spins without using the **Set Wheel Speed** block? How many blocks would you need to use so that Dash spins in a full circle in each loop?

Cross-Curricular Connections

MATH

- Have students run the program and count the number of circles that Dash makes to the left and right. Then have them represent the results as fractions (e.g., 3 and a half circles). (CCSS.MATH.2.G.A.3)

- Have students change the number of repeats in the program (e.g., Repeat 2 times). Then have them record the number of circles that Dash makes with the new settings. Have students repeat this process several times. Finally, have students represent their results with a picture graph or bar graph. (CCSS.MATH.2.MD.D.10)

ELA

- Have students write an opinion piece about whether they think Dash should try to stop the spaceship from spinning, call for help, or jump out of the spaceship. Encourage them to provide reasons for their arguments. (E.g., "Dash should call for help because it's safer than jumping out of the spaceship and other people might know what to do to stop the spaceship.") (CCSS.ELA.W.2.1)

- Have students write dialogue for Dash to say during the beginning, middle, and end of the program. (E.g., "Whoa! What's going on?" or "Help! This is crazy!") Then have them use **My Sounds** blocks to record the dialogue and add it to the program. (CCSS.ELA.W.2.3)

NOTES:

C 3.2 Help, help, help!

Time: 10 minutes

Hints

- To get Dash to turn in a circle, the **left** and **right wheel speeds** must be different. Tap on the **Set Wheel Speed** block and use the dials on the bottom to set the speed of the left and right wheels.

- To turn left, the right wheel needs to be faster than the left wheel in the **Set Wheel Speed** block. To turn right, the left wheel needs to be faster than the right wheel.

- Put a **sound** block inside each **Repeat** block to make Dash call out for help after each spin.

Suggested Solution:

Discussion Questions

1. What would happen if the left and right wheels were going at the same speed? What would happen if one wheel were moving forward and one wheel were moving backward?

2. How could Dash use lights to get help? How would you change the program to add the lights?

Cross-Curricular Connections

- Have students run the program and count the number of circles that Dash makes to the left and right. Then have them represent the results as fractions (e.g., 3 and a half circles). (CCSS.MATH.2.G.A.3)

- Have students change the number of repeats in the program (e.g., Repeat 2 times). Then have them record the number of circles that Dash makes with the new settings. Have students repeat this process several times. Finally, have students represent their results with a picture graph or bar graph. (CCSS.MATH.2.MD.D.10)

ELA

- Have students devise a way to save Dash from the spinning spaceship (e.g., a robotic arm). Have them write a paragraph describing their idea and explaining the reasoning behind it, using supporting facts and details. (CCSS.ELA.W.2.2)

- Have students write a narrative about how Dash ended up on a broken spaceship. Encourage students to include descriptive details, such as how Dash found the spaceship and/or what made the spaceship spin out of control. (CCSS.ELA.W.2.3)

NOTES:

C | 3.3 Robot Rescue!

Time: 15 minutes

Hints

- For this program, you will need **2 different repeat** blocks. When do you need a **Repeat Forever** block and when do you need a **Repeat 3 Times** block?

- The **When** block helps Dash tell when something happens (e.g., such as being picked up). What should happen after Dash is picked up? What blocks do you need to put under the **When** block?

- To make sure Dash calls out for help after each spin, put a **sound** block inside the **Repeat Forever** block.

Suggested Solution:

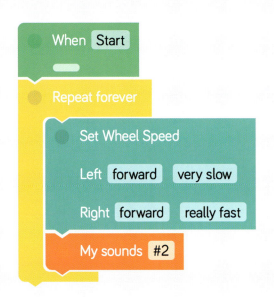

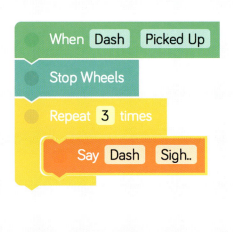

Discussion Questions

1. Why do you need to use the **Stop Wheels** block after Dash is picked up? How would you use the **Stop Wheels** block in other programs?

2. In this program, you needed **2 different repeat** blocks. Why couldn't you use the same **repeat** block? What would happen if both **repeat** blocks were **Repeat Forever** blocks?

Cross-Curricular Connections

- Have students create a number line from 0 to 30. Then have student volunteers stand on one side of the room and place Dash on the opposite side. Start the program and have student volunteers take turns racing to pick up Dash as quickly as possible. For each attempt, have the rest of the group/class count the number of times Dash makes full circles before being picked up. Have students record the results on the number line. (CCSS.MATH.2.MD.B.6)

- Have students write a narrative about what Dash does after being picked up and saved from the spinning spaceship. Does Dash go home? Does Dash fix the spaceship? Encourage students to use descriptive details. (CCSS.ELA.W.2.3)

NOTES:

D | 1.1

Cheer Up, Friends!

Time: 15 minutes

Hints

- Walk around in a square shape. Did you notice a pattern? Which directions did you need to turn? What blocks could help you repeat the pattern?

- Dash needs to use **Forward** and **Turn Left** blocks. How much does Dash need to move forward and turn left in order to get around the square?

- How can we help Dash repeat the dance **3 times** for each friend? If we used a **2nd Repeat** block, where would we put it?

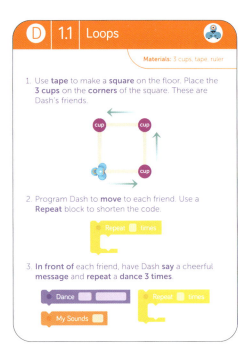

Suggested Solution:

97

Discussion Questions

1. Why did you need to use 2 **Repeat** blocks in order to make your program work?

2. Explain what would happen if the **second Repeat** block were below and not inside the first **Repeat** block.

3. Describe how the blocks might need to change if the shape were a rectangle.

Cross-Curricular Connections

- Have students measure out the square in centimeters. (CCSS.MATH.1.MD.A.2)

- Have students add up the total distance that Dash traveled in the challenge. (CCSS.MATH.1.OA.A.1)

- Have students turn the square into a map by adding features like a key and compass. (CCSS.ELA.RI.K.7)

- Have students write their own version of the challenge using a different story and objectives. (CCSS.ELA-LITERACY.W.1.7)

NOTES:

D | 1.2 Step It Up!

Time: 20 minutes

Hints

- Break up each event into smaller steps. Do you notice a pattern in the steps? What blocks could help you repeat the pattern?

- Dash needs to use **Forward** blocks and **Turn Right** blocks. How much does Dash need to move forward and turn right in order to get around the square?

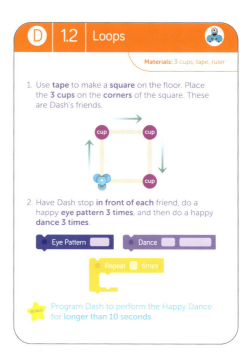

Suggested Solution:

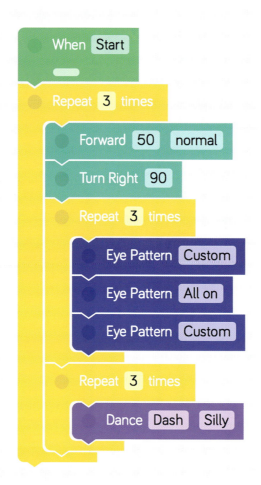

Discussion Questions

1. Why do you think Dash is so happy?

2. Explain where you think Dash learned those dance moves.

3. Describe what happens when the entire program is put inside another **Repeat** block.

Cross-Curricular Connections

- Have students measure each side of the square. Have them calculate the sum of the sides added together. (CCSS.MATH.K.OA.A.2)

- Have students find two objects in the room and compare the length of these objects to the sides of the square they made. Which one is the shortest? Which one is the longest? (CCSS.MATH.1.MD.A.1)

- Have students write a story about what happens after Dash finishes spreading happiness. (CCSS.ELA.W.1.3)

NOTES:

Happy Dance Flash Mob!

Time: 20 minutes

Hints

- Program Dash to do one part of the dance at a time. Then put all the parts together.

- Don't be afraid to be creative! Try using a variety of blocks, such as different **drive**, **look**, and **animation** blocks.

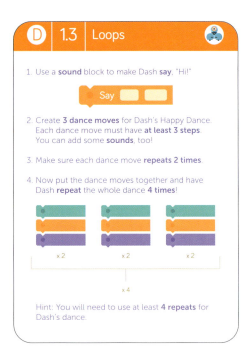

Suggested Solution:

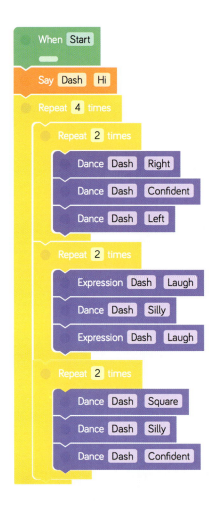

Discussion Questions

1. Describe what was easy about your coding experience and what was challenging.

2. What accessory could Dash use to make this dance more entertaining?

Cross-Curricular Connections

- Have students count how many times Dash does each dance and write the number down. Then have them change the number of repeats in each loop and count again.
  (CCSS.MATH.K.CC.B.5)

- Have students draw a picture of Dash dancing. Then have them explain what Dash is doing and why. (CCSS.ELA.W.K.2)

- Have students write a narrative recounting the sequence of Dash's dances.
  (CCSS.ELA.W.1.3)

NOTES:

D 2.1 Follow the Coach

Time: 10 minutes

Hints

- Make sure that Dash and Dot are both turned on and connected to the **Blockly** app.

- Dash should work out every time Dash sees Dot. Where should you put the **Forward** and **My Sounds** blocks to make sure that happens?

- Dash finds Dot best when Dot's eye is at the same level as Dash's. If necessary, place **books** underneath Dot to increase Dot's height. Also, put Dot far enough away so that Dash can see Dot's eye.

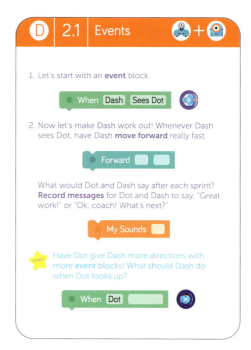

Suggested Solution:

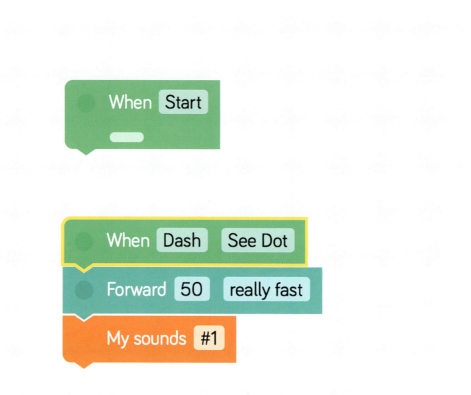

103

Discussion Questions

1. What other **event** blocks can Dot use to train Dash? What should Dash do when Dot **looks up**? What should Dash do when Dot **leans right**?

2. How does Dash sense Dot? (Answer: A signal is sent from the four pill-shaped black marks on Dot's body. The signal is sensed through Dash's eye.)

Cross-Curricular Connections

- Have students use Dot to make Dash move a certain number of times. Have students use multiplication to calculate how far Dash moved. Bonus: Have them display their calculations using an equation. (CCSS.MATH.3.OA.D.8)

- Have students write a paragraph describing what they imagine Dash's big event could be. Have them provide reasons why they think Dot needs to train Dash for the big event. (CCSS.ELA.W.3.1)

NOTES:

D | 2.2 Training Day

Time: 15 minutes

Hints

- There should be **at least 1 Repeat** block for each event. What do you want Dash to repeat? Place those blocks **inside** the **Repeat** block.

- Make sure that Dash and Dot are both connected to the **Blockly** app.

Suggested Solution:

Discussion Questions

1. What other **event** blocks can Dot use to train Dash? What should Dash do when Dot **looks up**? What should Dash do when Dot **leans right**?

2. How could you make a workout for Dash that uses a **nested loop**?

Cross-Curricular Connections

- Have students multiply how many times Dash performs a certain type of block (e.g., **light** blocks, **drive** blocks) by the number of **repeats** in each loop. Bonus: Have them express their calculations using equations. (CCSS.MATH.3.OA.D.8)

- Have students write, record, and/or perform a workout song for Dash's training. (CCSS.ELA.W.3.10)

NOTES:

D 2.3 The Big Event!

Time: 20 minutes

Hints

- When you're testing your program, make sure only one person is **calling out** "**Polo**!" or Dash will become confused.

- What block can you use so that Dash **turns toward** your voice? When should Dash **say**, "**Marco**!"? Hint: You can use the **sound** block more than once.

- If the classroom is very noisy, use the **Hear Clap** cue instead of the **Hear Voice** cue. You can also ask the teacher for permission to try out your program outside or in the hallway.

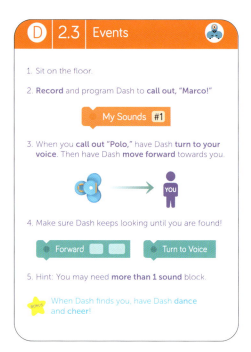

Suggested Solution:

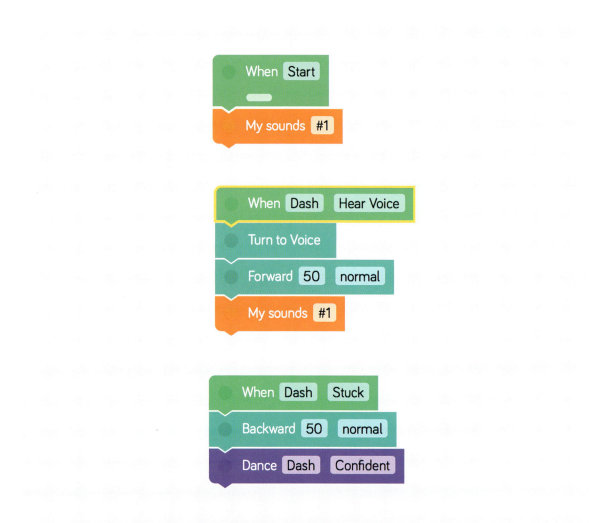

Discussion Questions

1. What was the trickiest part of the code for you to figure out? Was it getting Dash to turn to your voice? Why was it tricky and how did you solve the problem?

2. How could you add Dot to this game? How could Dot help Dash by using more **event** blocks?

Cross-Curricular Connections

- Have students calculate how far Dash needed to travel before finding the student. Bonus: Have them display their calculations using an equation. (CCSS.MATH.3.OA.D.8)

- Have students write about how they arrived at the solution. What did they try first? What did they do next? (CCSS.ELA.W.3.3.C)

NOTES:

D | 3.1 Fire Monster!

Time: 10-15 minutes

Hints

- Make sure to put the **Whistle** animation block **outside** the If block.

- To move Dash **really fast**, use the **Forward** block and turn the speed dial to the right.

Suggested Solution:

Discussion Questions

1. What happens if you put all of the code in a **Repeat Forever** block?

2. What if there were a Fire Monster **In Front** of Dash? How would you change the code to make it fit the new story?

Cross-Curricular Connections

- Call out a number between 1 and 100. Have students round this number to the nearest ten and program Dash to drive this far away from the Fire Monster. (CCSS.MATH.3.NBT.A.1)

- Have students write a story that describes the Fire Monster. What is its name? What does it eat? Where does it live? Should Dash be scared of the Fire Monster or is it friendly?
  (CCSS.ELA.W.3.3)

NOTES:

D | 3.2 Big and Scary!

Time: 15-20 minutes

Hints

- Make sure to put all the blocks that Dash needs to scare away the Fire Monster inside the **If** block.

- To get Dash to turn in a circle, the **left** and **right** **wheel speeds** must be different.

Suggested Solution:

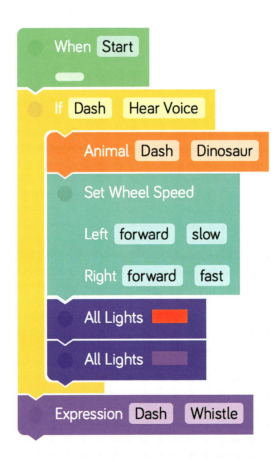

111

Discussion Questions

1. What combination of **wheel speeds** make Dash **turn left**? What combination of **wheel speeds** make Dash **turn right**?

2. **Conditionals** are blocks that help your robot make choices. In this case, **if** Dash hears a voice, Dash will turn in a circle and flash lights. However, **if** Dash does not hear a voice, Dash will calmly whistle. How could you change the program you used in this challenge so that **if** Dash hears the Fire Monster's voice, Dash acts friendly to it instead of trying to scare it away?

Cross-Curricular Connections

- In order to scare the Fire Monster, Dash must turn in at least one complete circle. Using the **Set Wheel Speed** block followed by a **Stop Wheels** block, have students create different combinations of wheel speeds (e.g., right wheel slow, left wheel really fast) and record what fraction of a circle Dash turns. To do this, have students draw a circle with a diameter of 40 cm on a piece of cardboard. Divide the circle into 10 equal parts. Place Dash in the center of the circle and see how many tenths Dash rotates. (CCSS.MATH.3.NF.A.1)

- Have students complete the previous activity and place the fractions they found on a number line. Students can also turn the fractions into decimals.
(CCSS.MATH.3.NF.A.2, CCSS.MATH.CONTENT.3.NF.A.3, CCSS.MATH.CONTENT.4.NF.C.6)

- Dash is trying to look big and scary so the Fire Monster will go away. This is Dash's defense against the Fire Monster. Research an animal and how it defends itself. Use Dash to demonstrate this defense to the class. (CCSS.ELA.W.3.7, CCSS.ELA.SL.3.1)

NOTES:

D | 3.3 Curious Fire Monster

Time: 30-35 minutes

Hints

- To save time, **record all 4 sounds** at one time.

- Before starting the program, put Dot in the first position you choose.

- You will need to use **4 If** blocks to complete this challenge.

Suggested Solution:

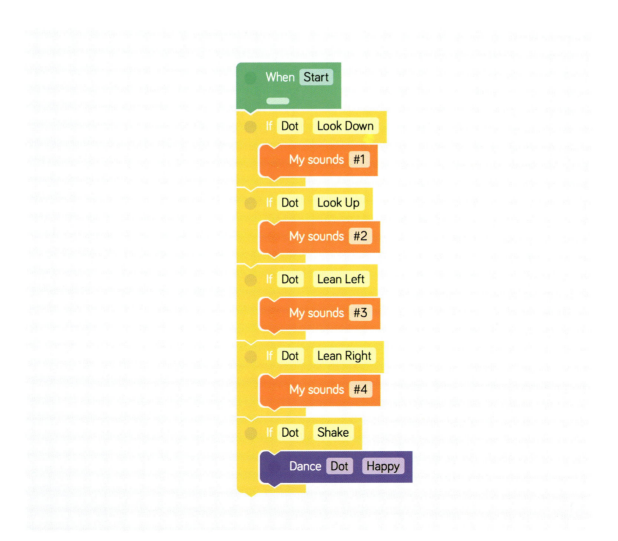

113

Discussion Questions

1. Why do you need to tilt Dot left or right or place Dot face down or face up before starting the program? What happens if you don't do this?

2. What other cues could you add to your program?

Cross-Curricular Connections

- Instead of recording 4 sounds, have students record 4 different numbers. Have them write a word problem that includes the 4 numbers in the order Dot gave them. Students must use at least 2 different operations (e.g., addition and multiplication, subtraction and multiplication, division and addition). Then have students solve each other's word problems.
(CCSS.MATH.3.OA.D.8)

- The Fire Monster was looking at Dot very closely. Now Dot is looking closely at the Fire Monster. What does Dot see? Have students draw a picture of the Fire Monster and then write a detailed description of what it looks like. Have them share their descriptions only with partners and have the partners draw what they think that Fire Monster looks like. Finally, have partners compare their drawings. Students can also use Dot to record their Fire Monster descriptions. Then students can play Dot's descriptions for their partners.
(CCSS.ELA.W.3.10, CCSS.ELA.L.3.1)

NOTES:

D | 3.4 The Dot Monster

Time: 10 minutes

Hints

- Make sure that Dash and Dot are both turned on and connected to the **Blockly** app.

- Dash finds Dot best when Dot's eye is at the same level as Dash's. If necessary, place **books** underneath Dot to increase Dot's height. Also, put Dot far enough away so that Dash can see Dot's eye.

- The **If** block has a C shape. That means you put blocks inside it. Those blocks will only function **if** Dash sees Dot.

Suggested Solution:

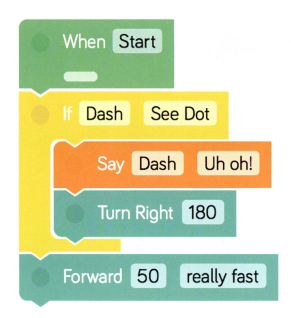

Discussion Questions

1. What if Dash doesn't see the Dot monster? What will Dash do?

2. How could you use a loop so that Dash looks for the Dot monster more than once?

Cross-Curricular Connections

- Have students use **2 turn** blocks to make Dash rotate **180 degrees**. Have them record the angle combinations that were successful (e.g., 120 degrees + 60 degrees). (CCSS.MATH.4.MD.C.5)

- Have students write a "backstory" for the Dot monster. Where did the Dot monster come from? Why does the Dot monster want to chase Dash? (CCSS.ELA.W.3.3)

NOTES:

D 3.5 Dash's Escape!

Time: 15 minutes

Hints

- You may need to use **more than 1 if** block to complete the challenge.

- If Dash doesn't react to the objects used to represent trees, use taller objects so that Dash can sense them.

- Put the objects **close together** so that Dash can sense them no matter which way Dash is turned. You may need to adjust the position of the objects a few times.

Suggested Solution:

117

Discussion Questions

1. How could a **loop** help Dash escape using fewer blocks? Do you see a pattern of blocks that repeat more than once?

2. How could you add the Dot monster to the program? What could Dot do to scare Dash while Dash tries to escape the forest?

Cross-Curricular Connections

- Have students calculate how many total degrees Dash needs to turn, based on what "tree" Dash is facing in the beginning (e.g., 90 degrees, 180 degrees, 270 degrees). (CCSS.MATH.4.MD.C.5)

- Have students write and record dialogue for Dash to say at the beginning and end of the program. The dialogue can describe Dash's feelings or what Dash is seeing in the forest during and after the escape. (CCSS.ELA.W.3.3)

NOTES:

D | 3.6 Dash Escapes Again

Time: 20 minutes

Hints

- You may need to use several **if** and **repeat** blocks to complete the challenge.

- If Dash doesn't react to the objects used to represent walls, use taller objects so that Dash can sense them.

- Put the objects **close together** so that Dash can sense them no matter which way Dash is turned. You may need to adjust the position of the objects a few times.

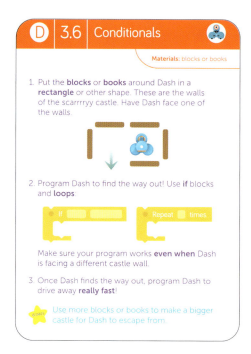

Suggested Solution:

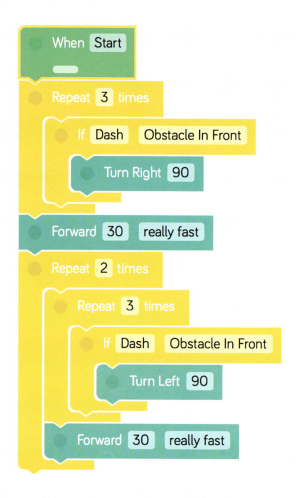

Discussion Questions

1. How could you use **When** blocks to complete the challenge?

2. How could you use the **Wonder** app to complete it? How is the **Wonder** app solution different from your **Blockly** app solution?

3. How could you add the Dot monster to the program? What could Dot do to scare Dash while Dash tries to escape the castle?

Cross-Curricular Connections

- Have students calculate how many total degrees Dash turned during the program, based on what "wall" Dash is facing in the beginning (e.g., 90 degrees, 180 degrees, 270 degrees). (CCSS.MATH.4.MD.C.5)

- Have students write and record dialogue for Dash to say at the beginning and end of the program. The dialogue can describe Dash's feelings or what Dash is seeing in the castle during and after the escape. (CCSS.ELA.W.3.3)

NOTES:

Rootin' Tootin' Line Dance!

Time: 15-20 minutes

Hints

- Look for the **Repeat Until** block in the **Control** menu.

- If you use **turn** blocks in your line dance, include a **left** and **right turn** block and make sure they have the same number.

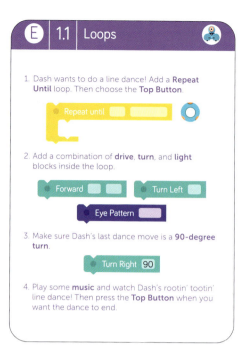

Suggested Solution:

Discussion Questions

1. What are some examples of line dances that you know (e.g., Chicken Dance, Cupid Shuffle)? How are these dances similar and/or different to the one that you programmed for Dash?

2. Why do you think each loop ends with a 90-degree turn in a line dance? If each person completes 4 loops of a line dance, what shape will they create when they are finished?

Cross-Curricular Connections

- Have students use a different degree angle at the end of each loop. Make sure they keep the angles equal and that their sum is 360 degrees. How many loops does Dash need to complete a full circle if the angle degree changes? (CCSS.MATH.4.MD.C.6)

- Have students write a paragraph teaching another student how to do Dash's line dance. To add another level of fun, have students read their paragraphs out loud while the other students do the dance. (CCSS.ELA.W.4.4, CCSS.ELA.W.4.10)

NOTES:

E | 1.2 Dance Along with Dot!

Time: 20 minutes

Hints

- Record your dance moves with the **My Sounds** block. **Record a New Sound** for each numbered slot.

- Make sure the dance moves you record are short enough so that you can finish each one before Dot moves on to the next.

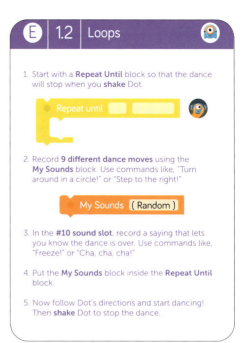

Suggested Solution:

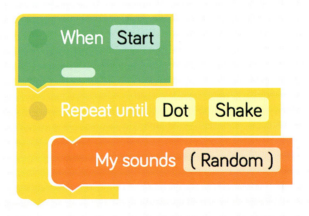

Discussion Questions

1. Can you use the **Random Sounds** block to program and play a different game?

2. What happens when you use the **Random Sounds** block but do not record sounds for every slot?

Cross-Curricular Connections

MATH

- Have students use the **Repeat Until Hear Clap** block and have them record a variety of numbers (1-9). Have students practice adding or multiplying the digits that Dot calls out. They can take turns making Dot stop by applauding. (CCSS.MATH.1.OA.C.6. CCSS.MATH.3.OA.C.7)

ELA

- Have the class collaborate to write several story starters. Have students record the story starters with the **My Sounds** block. Then, have them play the program until they hear the story starter they like best and shake Dot to stop the process. Finally, have them use the story starter to write a narrative. (CCSS.ELA.W.3.3)

- Have students record superlative and comparative sentences (e.g., "He runs the fastest," or "Her room is cleaner."). Have students identify each sentence according to its type. (CCSS.ELA.L.3.1)

NOTES:

E | 1.3 Dance Machine Dash!

Time: 30-35 minutes

Hints

- Use the **Repeat Until** block found in the **Control** menu.

- You will need at least **4 Repeat Until** blocks for all of the different events. Program a different dance for each **Repeat Until** block.

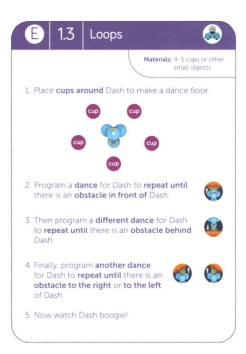

Suggested Solution:

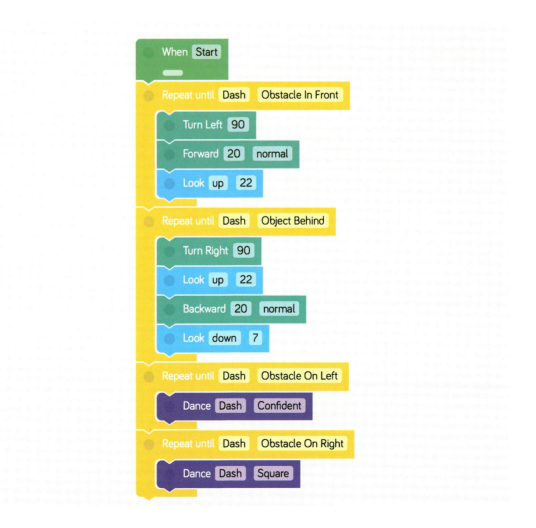

Discussion Questions

1. What other **Repeat Until** block cues could you use for your dance? Could you use a **Hear Clap** or **Hear Voice** cue?

2. Could you add a different kind of loop within the **Repeat Until** loop?

Cross-Curricular Connections

- Have students add **Repeat Until Button 1, Repeat Until Button 2,** and **Repeat Until Button 3** blocks. Program Dash to make a different shape for each button (e.g., create a square until they press Button 1). The complexity of this exercise could be increased by changing the required shapes. Students can also determine the perimeter and area of each shape. (CCSS.MATH.4.MD.C.5, CCSS.MATH.4.MD.A.3)

ELA

- Have students research an inventor and how that person finally got one of his or her inventions to work. Have students describe how creating this program is similar to creating a new invention (e.g., the inventor reaches an obstacle and has to find a way to work around it). This would also be a good analogy to use to spark a discussion about obstacles in our own lives and how we overcome them. (CCSS.ELA.W.3.2)

NOTES:

E | 2.1 Follow the Leader

Time: 10 minutes

Hints

- Use the **If/Else** block and choose **If Dash Object Behind**.

- Place the **Forward** block **inside** the If portion of the **If/Else** block.

- Be sure to place the **If/Else** block inside a **Repeat Forever** block.

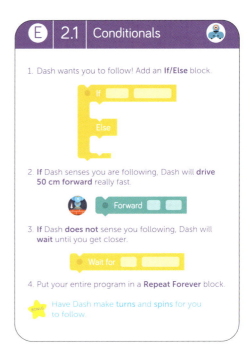

Suggested Solution:

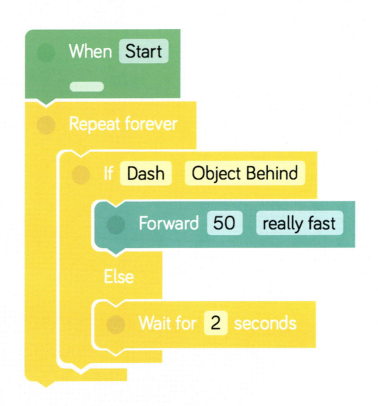

Discussion Questions

1. If you wanted Dash to add turns for you to follow, where would you place them in the code?

2. Could Dash play Follow the Leader if you were the leader? How would you have to change the program to make this work?

Cross-Curricular Connections

MATH

- Have students program Dash to drive a variety of distances. Have them record each distance as two different fractions: one with a denominator of 100 and one with a denominator of 10 (e.g., 20/100 and 2/10). (CCSS.MATH.4.NF.C.5)

ELA

- Have students work in pairs and play Follow the Leader using words. Have students take turns being the leader and the follower. The leader must say an adjective. The follower must say a synonym. Continue the game until one person can't think of another synonym for that word. To play this game with Dash, have students record 10 different adjectives. Have them program Dash to play one of the recordings randomly. Then have students take turns calling out a synonym of the recorded adjective. (CCSS.ELA.L.4.5.C)

NOTES:

E | 2.2 GOOOOOAL!!!

Time: 25-30 minutes

Hints

- Make sure that Dash and Dot are both turned on and connected to the **Blockly** app.

- Dash finds Dot best when Dot's eye is at the same level as Dash's. If necessary, place **books** underneath Dot to increase Dot's height. Also, put Dot far enough away so that Dash can see Dot's eye.

- Conditional blocks help robots make choices. In this case, **if** Dash sees Dot, Dash will try to distract Dot with lights and sounds. Or **else**, Dash will score a goal.

Suggested Solution:

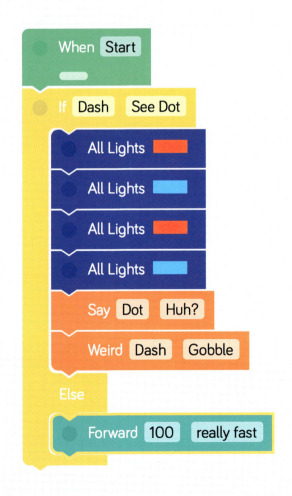

Discussion Questions

1. Why do you have to turn on Dot in order for Dash to see Dot?

2. How could we make Dash try to score another goal? Where would you put the **Repeat** block?

Cross-Curricular Connections

- Have students solve the following word problem: If the goal were 8,000 cm away from Dash, how many times would you have to program Dash to **drive 100 cm forward** in order to score a goal? (CCSS.MATH.4.NBT.A.1)

- Have students discuss the following question with a partner or in small groups: Dash needs to make it past a goalie in order to score a point. Have you ever had to get through an obstacle in order to achieve something in your life? (CCSS.ELA.W.4.3)

NOTES:

E | 2.3 Ready or Not!

Time: 40-45 minutes

Hints

- Make sure that Dash and Dot are both turned on and connected to the **Blockly** app.

- Dash finds Dot best when Dot's eye is at the same level as Dash's. Also, put Dot far enough away so that Dash can see Dot's eye.

- The program does not run effectively when all the **Drive** and **Turn** blocks are placed inside one **If/Else** block. If you do this, Dash will only try to see Dot one time, facing the same direction each time. By placing one movement inside each **If/Else** Block, you ensure that Dash tries to see Dot after every move.

- Make sure that Dash drives forward a small amount at a time. If Dash drives too far, Dash may miss Dot.

Suggested Solution:

Discussion Questions

1. With this program, would Dash still be able to find Dot if Dot were moved to a different hiding spot? Why or why not?

2. Would this program work if Dot were hiding under a blanket or behind a box? Why or why not?

Cross-Curricular Connections

MATH

- Have students predict how far away Dash needs to be in order to detect Dot. Use rulers to make exact predictions. Run the program several times, placing Dot in a variety of locations. Measure the distances from which Dash sensed Dot each time. Were your predictions correct? (CCSS.MATH.4.MD.A.1)

ELA

- Have students play Hide and Seek with a partner. Have them take turns hiding an object (or Dot) in the classroom. Their goal is to help their partner find the object as quickly as possible without speaking. Have students write clues to their partner about where the object is located using complete sentences with proper capitalization and punctuation. (CCSS.ELA.L.4.6)

NOTES:

E | 3.1 Dance Rehearsal

Time: 15 minutes

Hints

- To create a function, start a new stack with the **Function** block and put blocks inside of it. Then use the **Call Function** block to have Dash perform the function during your program.

- You can name your function by tapping on the **Function** block.

Suggested Solution:

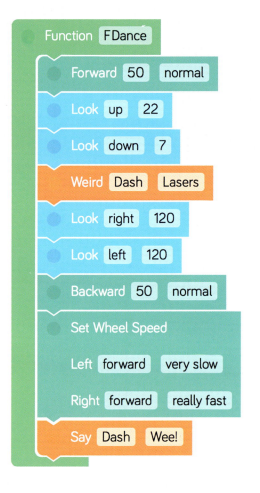

Discussion Questions

1. Why do you think a function was used in this program? How did the function make the program more efficient?

2. How could you add another function to the program? What dance move would you want Dash to do using the new function?

Cross-Curricular Connections

- Have students program a function to make Dash follow a square, triangle, or rectangle path. Then have them identify the size of the angles in each shape and calculate how many total degrees Dash turned during each program. (CCSS.MATH.4.G.A.1)

- Have students write, perform and/or record a song for Dash's performance. (CCSS.ELA.W.4.10)

NOTES:

E | 3.2 Fancy Wheelwork

Time: 20 minutes

Hints

- To create a function, start a new stack with the **Function** block and put blocks inside of it. Then use the **Call Function** block to have Dash perform the function during your program.

- To make sure Dash dances at each corner of the square path, use the **Call Function** block before or after each of Dash's turns.

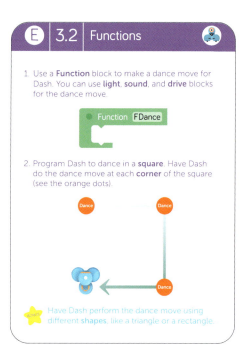

Suggested Solution:

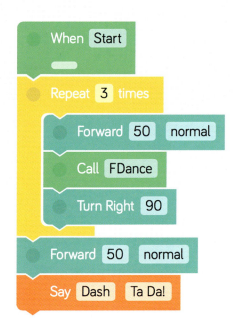

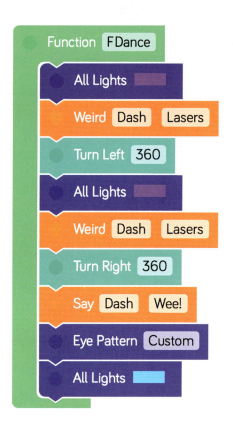

Discussion Questions

1. Why do you think a function was used in this program? How did the function make the program more efficient?

2. What function could help Dash make **more than 1** square path in the dance?

Cross-Curricular Connections

- Have students identify the size of the angles in the square. Then have them calculate how many total degrees Dash turned during the program (including the dance moves in each corner). (CCSS.MATH.4.G.A.1)

- Have students write, perform, and/or record a song for Dash's performance. (CCSS.ELA.W.4.10)

NOTES:

Dance Off!

Time: 25 minutes

Hints

- If you have more than one function in your program, tap the **Call Function** block to choose which function you want to use.

- How could you create a function for Dash to move in 1 **square pattern**? How could you use the function to help Dash make 4 **squares**?

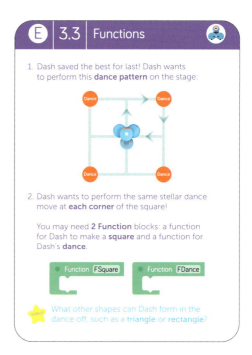

Suggested Solution:

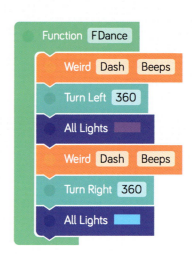

Discussion Questions

1. How many functions did you use in your program? Why did you create those functions?

2. What kinds of patterns could Dash make with triangle or rectangle paths (e.g., triangles that form squares or pinwheel patterns; rectangles that form brick or other tessellation patterns)?

3. What could you do to make Dash alternate between performing 2 different dance moves at the corners of the squares?

Cross-Curricular Connections

- Have students identify the size of the angles in the squares. Then have them calculate how many total degrees Dash turned during the program (including the dance moves in each corner). (CCSS.MATH.4.G.A.1)

- Have students write, perform, and/or record a song for Dash's performance. (CCSS.ELA.W.4.10)

NOTES:

E | 3.4 Dog Trainer

Time: 10-15 minutes

Hints

- To name a function, tap on the name, erase the word "Function," and add your own title. The "F" in Function does not delete, so all your function names will begin with an "F."

- Set each wheel at a different speed in order to get Dash to spin in a circle.

- To choose which function to call, tap on the **Call** block and select the function you want to use from the menu.

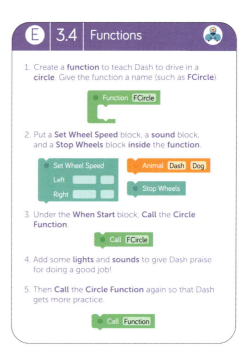

Suggested Solution:

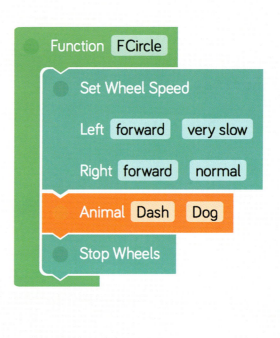

139

Discussion Questions

1. A **function** is a coding shortcut. Instead of writing the entire code sequence each time you want to use it, you can create a function. Whenever you're ready to use the coding sequence, just use the **Call** block. When is it helpful to use a function instead of a **Repeat** or **When** block?

2. What other tricks would you like Dash to perform? What kind of **functions** would you need to make for each trick? What blocks would you use?

Cross-Curricular Connections

- Have students add functions that make Dash turn 5 full circles. Then have students try making Dash turn 10 full circles. (CCSS.MATH.4.MD.C.5.A)

- Make Dash's trick more complicated by using the **Set Wheel Speed** and **Stop Wheel** blocks and having Dash turn a specific number of degrees. (CCSS.MATH.4.MD.C.5.A)

- Have students research techniques used to train two different animals. Have them write a composition comparing and contrasting the techniques. Then have them write a function to demonstrate Dash completing a trick after successful training techniques had been used. Finally, have students write a different function showing how Dash would complete a trick if the training techniques used were unsuccessful. (CCSS.ELA.W.4.2)

NOTES:

E | 3.5

Tricks Galore

Time: 20-25 minutes

Hints

- Sometimes Dash likes to be funny and do the unexpected. When you program the **Speak Function**, have Dash speak words in addition to barking.

- To make Dash's lights flash, add a **Repeat** block inside the **Function** block.

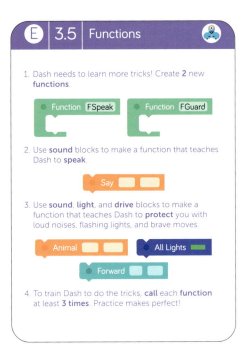

Suggested Solution:

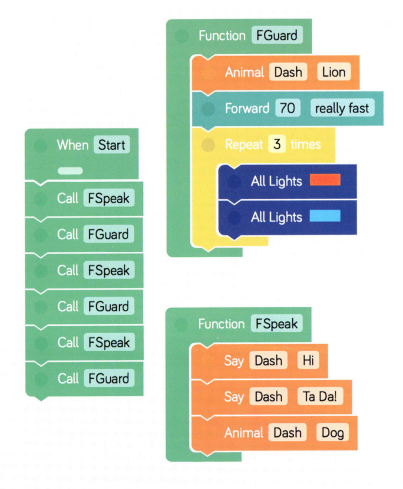

141

Discussion Questions

1. What would this program look like if you did not use functions?
2. How could you teach Dash a third or fourth trick? Would this be difficult or easy to do?

Cross-Curricular Connections

- Have students calculate the number of centimeters Dash travels during this challenge. Then have them change the number of centimeters Dash drives in the **Function Guard** block and solve the equation again. (CCSS.MATH.4.NBT.A.1)

- Have students record sentences using sound blocks and include them in a function to train Dash about the differences between to, too, and two. (E.g., He went to the pet store. I went there too. We got two treats for Dash.) Have them write another function to help Dash learn about the differences between there, their, and they're. (CCSS.ELA.L.4.1.G)

NOTES:

E | 3.6 Obstacle Course!

Time: 50-60 minutes

Hints

- Have Dash move slowly and in small increments to get around each circle.

- You might need to add **Drive** and **Turn** blocks between functions to get Dash to the proper starting point for each obstacle.

- Since the functions are already written, it's easy to add more of the same obstacles to your course in any order you choose.

Suggested Solution:

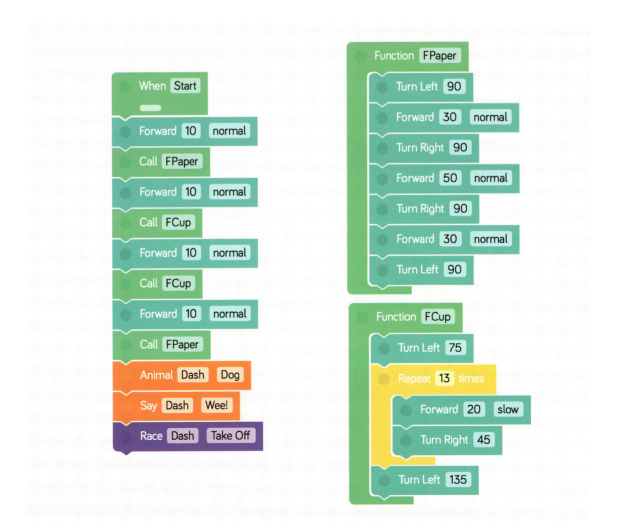

143

Discussion Questions

1. How would you need to change your program if you wanted to change the order of the obstacles in your course?

2. What other obstacles could you add? What functions would you need to program to go around each of the new obstacles?

Cross-Curricular Connections

- Have students write an equation showing the total number of centimeters Dash traveled in this challenge. Students must use both multiplication and addition.
  (CCSS.MATH.4.NBT.B.4, CCSS.MATH4.NBT.B.5)

- Have students drive Dash through the obstacle course 2 times. Have students modify the equation they created for the first math extension to calculate the new total number of centimeters Dash traveled. (CCSS.MATH.4.NBT.B.4, CCSS.MATH4.NBT.B.5)

- Have students work in pairs. Have pairs take turns creating obstacle courses for their partners using classroom objects (e.g., chairs, desks, backpacks, etc.). Make sure their partners face away from them or cover their eyes so they can't see the obstacle course until later in the activity. Then have students write a paragraph that tells their partner how to get through the obstacle course. Have the partners read the paragraph before walking through the obstacle course with their eyes closed. After the activity, have students evaluate how well they wrote the directions in their paragraphs and how they could improve them. (CCSS.ELA.L.4.3)

NOTES:

F | 1.1 Dash-chund

Time: 15 minutes

Hints

- First, the program needs to detect whether there is an object behind Dash. The first **If** block checks for that event. Then the second **If** block checks to see if Dash is being picked up.

- Make sure the the second **If** block is **inside** the first **If** block. That way, Dash will only sigh and greet you when there is both an obstacle behind Dash **AND** then Dash is picked up.

- Think about which **sound** blocks will best show that Dash is surprised or startled and which **sound** blocks will best show that Dash is relieved.

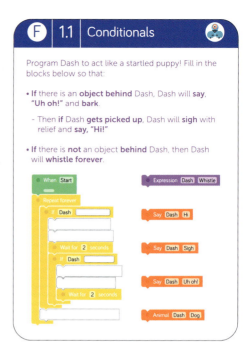

Suggested Solution:

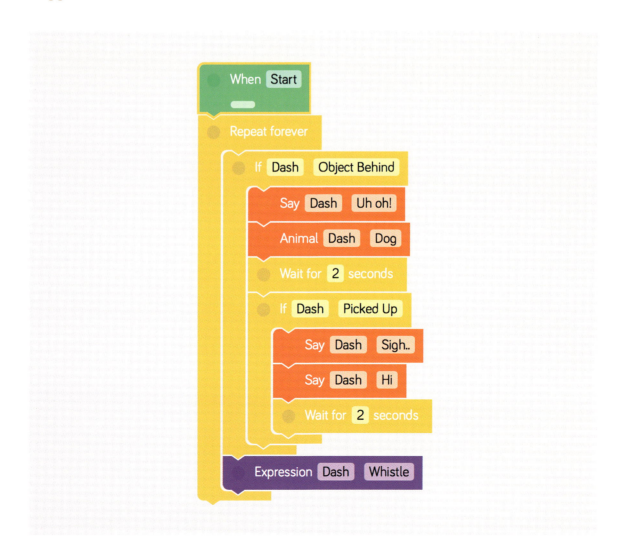

Discussion Questions

1. Why do you think we need the **Wait For** blocks at the end of each set of sound blocks?

2. What would happen if you put a third **If** block inside the second **If** block? What event could the program check for after Dash is picked up? Could it check to see if you're speaking?

Cross-Curricular Connections

MATH

- Have students measure how close they need to stand behind Dash in order to be detected. Then have them convert the measurement so that it's represented in inches, centimeters, and millimeters. Have students record their results. (CCSS.MATH.5.MD.A.1)

- On a gridded mat, have students make a coordinate system with x and y axes. Place Dash on the mat. Have students add a **Forward** block after the **Whistle** block in the program. This will make Dash move each time Dash whistles. Have students play the program and record Dash's coordinate location after each loop. (CCSS.MATH.5.G.A.1)

ELA

- Have students write about the challenge's story from a puppy's perspective. How does the puppy feel when someone sneaks up from behind it? Then how does the puppy feel when it's picked up? (CCSS.ELA.W.5.3)

NOTES:

F | 1.2 Ruff, ruff!

Time: 15 minutes

Hints

- First, use a **Function** block to program Dash to perform a spinning trick. Use the **Set Wheel Block** and set the right and left wheels to spin at different speeds.

- For each **If** block, use a **Call Function** block to make Dash perform the trick.

- Make sure the the second **If** block is **inside** the first **If** block. That way, Dash will only perform the extra animation if there is an obstacle in front of Dash **twice** in a row.

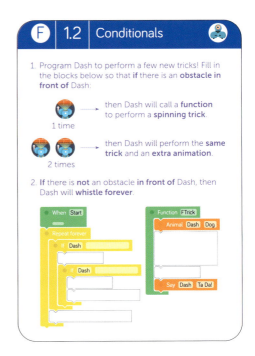

Suggested Solution:

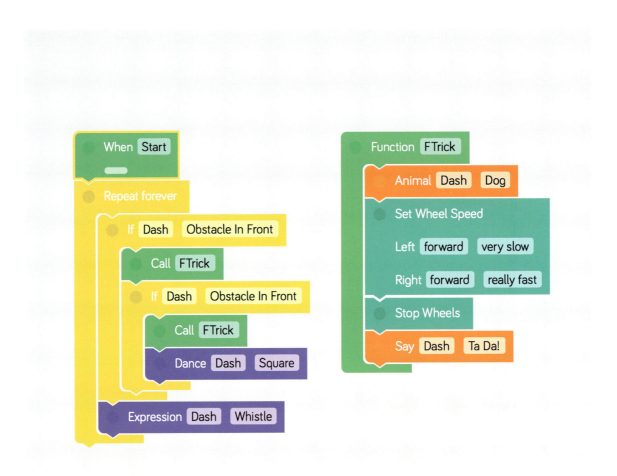

Discussion Questions

1. How does the **Function** block help improve your program? Does it make your program more efficient? Does it help you complete the program faster?

2. What would happen if you put a third **If** block inside the second **If** block? Could Dash perform another trick? If so, what trick would you want Dash to perform?

Cross-Curricular Connections

- Have students measure how close they need to stand in front of Dash in order to be detected. Then have them convert the measurement so that it's represented in inches, centimeters, and millimeters. Have students record their results. (CCSS.MATH.5.MD.A.1)

- Have students research and write about different strategies that trainers use to teach dogs new tricks (e.g., clicker training, positive reinforcement). Then have them program Dash to demonstrate these strategies. (CCSS.ELA.W.5.2)

- Have students write a narrative about what would happen if Puppy Dash threw up. Would Dash need to go to the hospital? Would Dash need to drink water or go outside? Then have them program Dash to act out the story. (CCSS.ELA.W.5.3)

NOTES:

F | 1.3 Nom, nom, nom!

Time: 20 minutes

Hints

- Use a **Function** block to program Dash to eat. Put the **Function** block next to the **When Start** block and add **Look** and **My Sounds** blocks to make Dash pretend to eat. Now, you can use the **Call Function** block each time you want Dash to eat.

- Make sure the the second **If** block is **inside** the first **If** block. That way, Dash will only **burp** if there is an obstacle in front of Dash **twice** in a row.

- Make sure the the third **If** block is **inside** the second **If** block. That way, Dash will only **throw up** if there is an obstacle in front of Dash **3 times** in a row.

Suggested Solution:

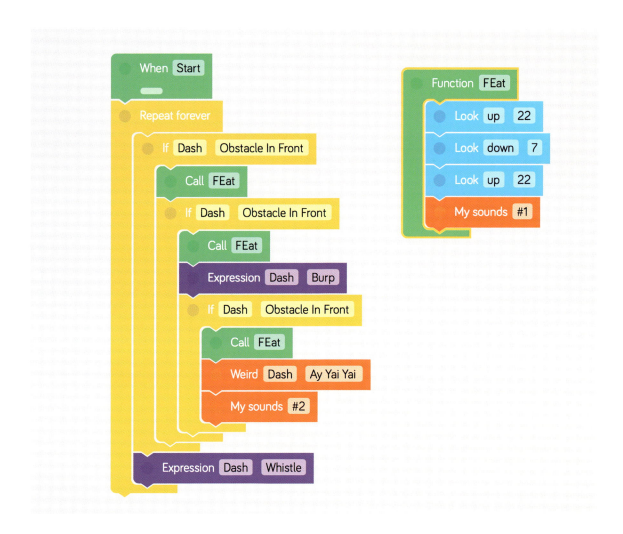

Discussion Questions

1. How does the **Function** block help you improve your program? Does it make your program more efficient? Does it help you complete the program faster?

2. What if you replaced one of the **If** blocks with a **When** block? How would that change the program? How would Dash's behavior change?

Cross-Curricular Connections

- Have students record the degrees Dash's head turns up or down in each of the **Look** blocks. Then have them calculate the total sum of the angles that Dash's head moves during the program. (CCSS.MATH.4.MD.C.5)

- Have students change the program so that Dash forms different shapes (e.g., square, rectangle, triangle). Then have them compare and contrast the code they used to form the different shapes. (CCSS.MATH.5.G.B.3)

ELA

- Have students research and write about proper eating habits for puppies (e.g., what they should eat, how much they should eat). Then have them program Dash to demonstrate their findings. For example, Dash could react to different types of food props depending on whether they're healthy for puppies (e.g., candy versus chicken). (CCSS.ELA.W.5.2)

NOTES:

F | 2.1 Road Trip!

Time: 15 minutes

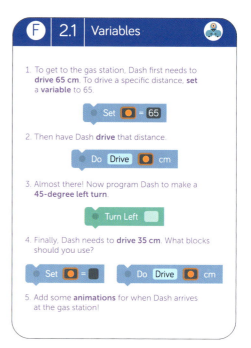

Hints

- You can find the **Set Variable** block and the **Do Drive Variable** block in the **Variables** menu.

- **Variables** allow us to store specific information in a program. In the **Blockly** app, the variables are represented by different fruits: orange, banana, apple, cherry, and watermelon.

- Make sure you use the same variable for the **Do Drive Variable** and **Set Variable** blocks.

- You will need **2 Set Variable** and **2 Do Drive Variable** blocks for this program because Dash needs to travel **2 distances**.

Suggested Solution:

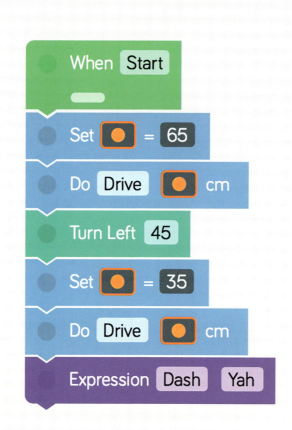

151

Discussion Questions

1. What if you wanted to use a different variable to set the **35 cm distance** in the challenge? How would you change the program to include a second variable?

2. How could variables be used in other programs? For example, how could you use variables to keep track of how often something happens to Dash or Dot?

Cross-Curricular Connections

- Have students use a coordinate grid to mark Dash's starting point and the location of the gas station. Then have them plot out a path from Dash to the gas station and use coordinate numbers to describe the route. (CCSS.MATH.5.G.A.1)

- Have students design a new path to the gas station using at least 2 acute turns and 2 obtuse turns. Then have them calculate the sum of all of the angles Dash turned on the path. (CCSS.MATH.4.MD.C.5, CCSS.MATH.4.MD.C.6, CCSS.MATH.4.MD.C.7)

- Have students write a narrative that describes why and where Dash is going on the big road trip. Encourage them to use descriptive and sensory details. (CCSS.ELA-W.5.3)

NOTES:

F 2.2 Pump It Up!

Time: 20 minutes

Hints

- To change the variable, tap the **Change Variable** block and enter **13** into the number pad.

- To select **Eye Light On**, tap on the **Do** block and select the last item. Then Dash's eye lights will show the variable number.

- Make sure you use the same variable for the **Change Variable**, **Do Eye Light On Variable**, **Do Drive Variable**, and **Set Variable** blocks.

Suggested Solution:

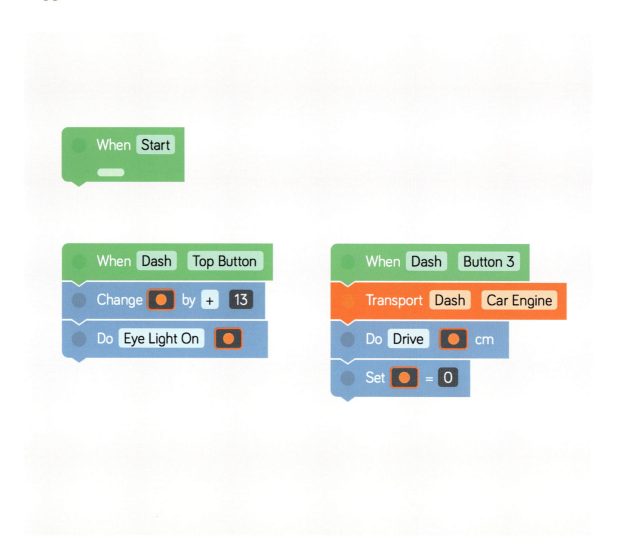

Discussion Questions

1. The **Do Eye Light On** Variable block uses Dash's eye lights to show the variable number. Why do you think the challenge has us add **13** to the variable each time the **Top Button** is pressed? (Hint: There are 12 eye lights. Each eye light represents a number. The top light represents the number 0 and then increases clockwise. The **Do Eye Light On Variable** block divides the **variable** by 12 and shows the remainder. For example, when the variable is 13, 13 ÷ 12 = 1 with a remainder of 1. Thus, the eye light for 1 is turned on.)

2. What would happen if you changed the variable using a different operator (e.g., subtraction, multiplication, division)? How would it affect the way Dash moved after **Button 3** is pressed?

Cross-Curricular Connections

- Give students random numbers between 13-900. Then have them predict how the eye light pattern will display each of the numbers, given that the **Do Eye Light On Variable** block divides the variable by 12 and shows the remainder. (CCSS.MATH.5.G.A.1)

- Have students press the **Top Button** 10 times and record the variable number each time. Then have them predict the values of the next 10-20 presses. Students can check their answers by running the program. (CCSS.MATH.5.OA.B.3)

ELA

- In real life, Dash runs on electric power, but in the story, Dash runs on gas. Have students write an opinion piece about the pros and cons of using electric versus gas-powered vehicles. (CCSS.ELA.W.5.1)

- Have students write a narrative that describes a road trip they've taken. If the students haven't been on a road trip, have them describe where they would go and what they would do on a dream road trip. Encourage them to use descriptive and sensory details. (CCSS.ELA.W.5.3)

NOTES:

F 2.3 On the Road!

Time: 25 minutes

Hints

- Use **Challenge Card F 2.2** to help you set up this program.

- To change the variable, tap the **Change Variable** block. Then you can add, subtract, multiply, or divide the variable. To **subtract**, tap the negative sign and then tap the number you want to subtract in the key pad.

- The **If Variable** block checks the value of the variable. Tap the **If Variable** block and change the operator to < in the menu. This will check if the variable is **less than 0**.

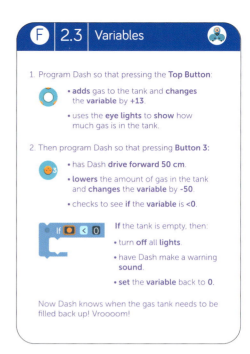

Suggested Solution:

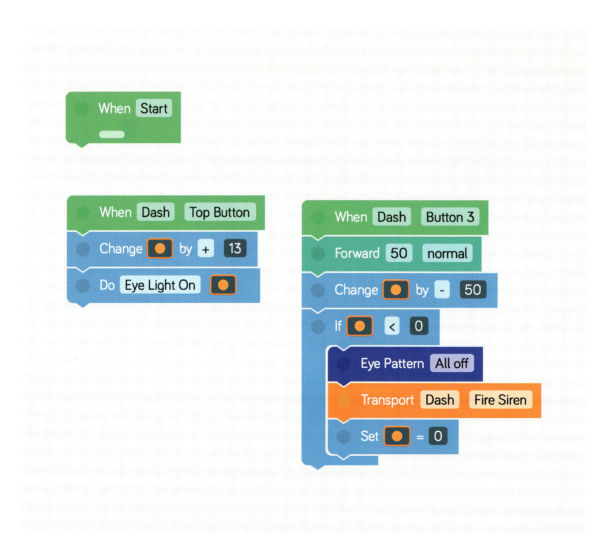

Discussion Questions

F | 2.3

1. Why do you need to **subtract 50** from the variable each time Dash moves **forward 50 cm**? How does this mimic the way gas is used to power cars?

2. How can you fill up Dash's gas tank faster? How would that change the way the eye lights show how much gas is in the tank?

Cross-Curricular Connections

MATH

- Give students random numbers between 13-900. Then have them predict how the eye light pattern will display each of the numbers, given that the **Do Eye Light On** block divides the variable by 12 and shows the remainder. (CCSS.MATH.5.NBT.B.6)

- Have students predict the value of the variable depending on the number of times Dash's **Top Button** and **Button 3** are pressed. (E.g., Top Button is pressed 9 times = variable of 117, Button 3 is pressed 2 times = variable of -100. Then the final value of the variable is 17.). (CCSS.MATH.5.OA.B.3)

ELA

- Have students research and write about how gas is used to power cars. Then have them describe how they would change Dash's program to better reflect the way gas is used by cars. (CCSS.ELA.W.5.2)

- Have students write a narrative about what they would do if they ran out of gas on a road trip and were far away from any gas stations. Encourage them to use descriptive and sensory details. (CCSS.ELA.W.5.3)

NOTES:

Magic Dot Ball

Time: 20 minutes

Hints

- To set a **variable** to a **random number**, tap the **Set Variable** block and then touch the **dice**. You can then set the range for your random number.

- To change the **conditional value**, tap the **If Variable** block and then tap the **equals** sign. You can then select the number you want on the keypad.

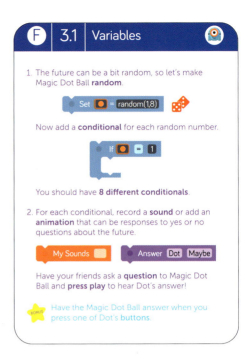

Suggested Solution:

157

Discussion Questions

1. What if you wanted Magic Dot Ball to have **10 different answers**? How would you change the program?

2. What if you wanted Magic Dot Ball to say "**yes**" when the variable was **even** and "**no**" when the variable was **odd**? How would you change the program?

Cross-Curricular Connections

- Have students play the program 15 times. Have them record which number the program randomly selects each time. Then have them graph and analyze what numbers came up most frequently. Have students play the program another 15 times and continue recording results to see how the graph changes. (CCSS.MATH.6.SP.B.5)

- Have students write and ask the Magic Dot Ball silly questions about their future and share the results of these questions to the class. Have them use details to describe the future that the Magic Dot Ball has chosen for them. (CCSS.ELA.SL.5.4)

NOTES:

F | 3.2 Duck, Dot, Goose!

Time: 20 minutes

Hints

- To set a **variable** to a **random number**, tap the **Set Variable** block and then touch the **dice**. You can then set the range for your random number.

- Decide how often Dot should **say** "**Duck**." For example, should Dot say "Duck" when the **variable** is **less than 4**? If so, what should Dot say when the **variable** is **greater than 4**?

Suggested Solution:

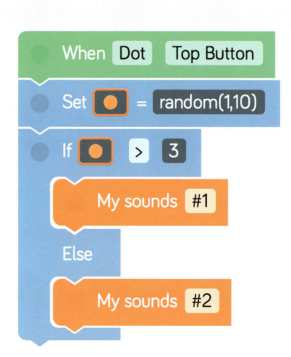

159

Discussion Questions

1. In your program, how long did it take for Dot to say "**Goose**?" How can you change the **randomness** and the **conditional** so that Dot says "Goose" more often?

2. What if you wanted Dot to say "**Duck**," "**Goose**," or "**Pigeon**?" How would you change the program to add a third word?

Cross-Curricular Connections

- Have students record how long it takes Dot to say "Goose" over the course of multiple games. Then have them graph their results and describe any overall patterns. (CCSS.MATH.6.SP.B.5)

- Have students program Dot to randomly say a transitional word (e.g., then, suddenly) instead of "Duck" or "Goose." Then have students make up a story as a group by passing Dot around and using Dot's randomly-generated transitional words to begin the next part of the story. (CCSS.ELA.W.5.3)

NOTES:

F 3.3 Win, Lose, or Dot!

Time: 30 minutes

Hints

- Since there are 2 different scores that you need to record, you'll need **2 variables**. Make sure you **set both variables to 0** at the beginning of each game.

- Use **When** and **Change Variable** blocks to add a point for Team 1 or 2. When Dot's **Top Button** is pressed, you will need an **If Variable** block to determine the winner.

Suggested Solution:

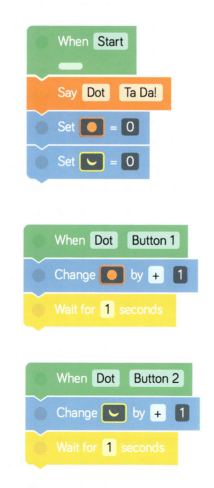

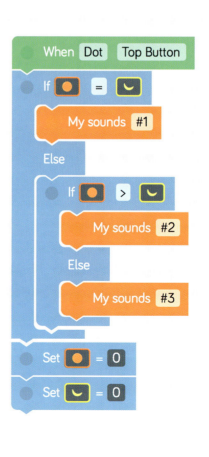

161

Discussion Questions

1. If the maximum score were **12**, how could you use Dot's **eye lights** to show a team's score? How many **conditionals** would you need to do this?

2. What if there were **3 teams** in the game? How could Dot keep track of 3 different scores?

Cross-Curricular Connections

- Have students program Dot so that each team's score is increased and then multiplied or divided each time that team's button is pressed (e.g., new score = (old score + 1) x 2). Then have students write a numerical expression showing the score change. (CCSS.MATH.5.OA.A.1)

- Have students present their program and explain how they arrived at their solution. Then have them demonstrate how to use the program in a simple game. (CCSS.ELA.SL.5.4)

NOTES:

F | 3.4 Lucky 7's

Time: 20-25 minutes

Hints

- Adjust the variable on the **Do Drive** block to the number of centimeters you want Dash to go.

- **Variables** allow us to store specific information in a program. In this program, we want to store 3 different numbers so we need **3 different variables**.

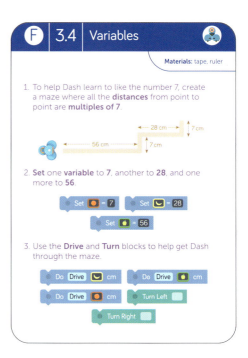

Suggested Solution:

Discussion Questions

1. If you wanted to make your maze bigger, what other multiples of 7 could you use?

2. How many variables can you add to one program? Why might you need more variables?

Cross-Curricular Connections

- Have students change the variables to be multiples of a different number. Students can share programs with one another and try to guess each other's numbers. (CCSS.MATH.4.OA.B.4)

- Have students calculate how many centimeters Dash would travel if this maze were 3 times as long. Then have them calculate the distance traveled if the maze were 5 times as long. (CCSS.MATH.4.OA.A.1)

- Have students write a narrative that tells why Dash did not like the number 7. What negative association did Dash have with the number 7? (CCSS.ELA.W.4.3)

NOTES:

13=Yuck

Time: 30-35 minutes

Hints

- The **Blockly** app labels variables with fruits. This helps you tell the variables apart.

- Add **2** additional **When** blocks and place them next to the **When Start** block. You will have 3 **columns** of code: one column of code beginning with the **When Start** block, one beginning with the **When Dot Move** block, and one beginning with the **When Dot Top Button** block.

Suggested Solution:

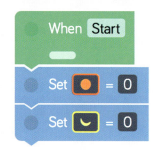

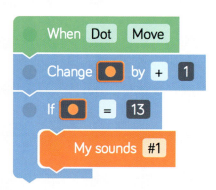

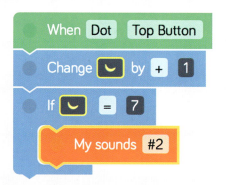

Discussion Questions

1. Try passing Dot without triggering the **move** cue. Does this work? Why or why not?

2. Could you get Dot to count by 7's? How?

Cross-Curricular Connections

- Have students write a rule (e.g., +3, -7, +1.25) and have them change the variable in the program using that rule. Have students work in pairs and try to guess the rule their partner made by playing the game with Dot. (CCSS.MATH.4.OA.C.5)

- Have students change the variable by a number other than 1. After testing the new variable in the program, have students create a multiplication array based on the new information. For example, if the variable changed by 3 and Dash moved 10 times during the game, the students should draw an array showing 10 groups of 3. (CCSS.MATH.4.OA.A.1)

- Dash and Dot are very superstitious. Have students think of a superstition that they know of or believe in. Then have them research the background of the superstition and why people started believing it to be true. Finally, have students share their findings with the class. (CCSS.ELA.RI.4.1)

NOTES:

F | 3.6 Black Cats!

Time: 35-40 minutes

Hints

- For this challenge, you will use **3 variables**.

- You will use the following **3 when** blocks:
    - Dash **Obstacle in Front**
    - Dash **Obstacle Behind**
    - Dash **Top Button**

- After each **When** block, add a **Change** Variable block and set the variable to increase by **1** whenever the event occurs.

- After each variable changes, use an **If/Else** or **If** Variable block to check the value of the variable.

- When the **Top Button** has been pressed 7 times, don't forget to use a **Go to Start** block. This will make all the variables reset to **0**.

Suggested Solution:

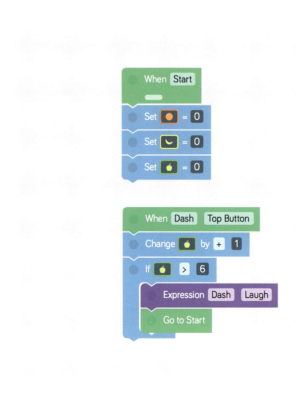

Discussion Questions

1. Using variables is helpful in this challenge. Why? Could we complete this challenge without using variables?

2. Why is using < and > useful in this challenge?

3. What happens if we <u>don't</u> use a **Go to Start** block when the **Top Button** is pressed 7 times?

Cross-Curricular Connections

- Have students run the program 5 times. Each time, have students measure how far Dash traveled and record the distance in inches. When students have run the program 5 times, have them add up the total number of inches Dash traveled and then determine how many feet Dash traveled. (CCSS.MATH.4.MD.A.2)

- Have students convert the number of centimeters Dash traveled into inches. (CCSS.MATH.5.MD.A.1)

- Have students write a narrative that tells why Dash is scared of black cats. What happened to Dash? (CCSS.ELA.W.4.3)

- Have students write a paragraph giving Dash strategies to overcome the fear of black cats. (CCSS.ELA.W.4.4)

NOTES:

Appendix

Digital PDFS of the following worksheets can be found on our website at:
education.makewonder.com/curriculum

Tips and Tricks Handout

K-2 Planning Worksheet for Dash

K-2 Planning Worksheet for Dot

3-5 Planning Worksheet

Challenge Card Checklists

Blockly Puzzle Tracker

Reflections Worksheet

Advanced Reflections Worksheet

Challenge Card Template

Troubleshooting Handout

Problem Solving & Debugging Handout

Evaluation Rubric

Challenge Card Tips & Tricks

 Determine Team Roles

Swap roles with your teammates for each challenge. Team roles include lead programmer, robot wrangler, and documentarian.

 Plan Your Path

Draw out the path you want Dash to follow. Then plan out the blocks you'll need. You can also get up and walk the path that you think Dash should take.

 Mark Your Spots

Use tape to mark Dash's starting spot and the location of any obstacles/objects.

 Go Back to Start

Always put Dash back at the starting spot before playing a program again.

 Use the When Start Block

Place your blocks under the **When Start** block. The **When Start** block should always be on your screen.

 Think in Centimeters

Dash moves in centimeters. A centimeter is about the width of your finger.

 Check Off the Steps

Use a dry erase marker to check off each step as you complete it. Make sure you erase the marks after you're done.

Help Your Robots Hear You

If the classroom is noisy, use the **Hear Clap** cue instead of the **Hear Voice** cue. Ask the teacher if you may try out your program with Dash and/or Dot outside or in the hallway.

Set a Time Limit

Give yourself or your team a set amount of time in which to complete the challenge

171

Dash Planning Worksheet

Name(s): _____   Date: _____

Coding Level: _____   Card #: _____

What do you want Dash to do?

Draw out the steps of the challenge or write a few sentences describing your goal.

Dot Planning Worksheet

Name(s): _____   Date: _____

Coding Level: _____   Card #: _____

What do you want Dot to do?
Draw out the steps of the challenge or write a few sentences describing your goal.

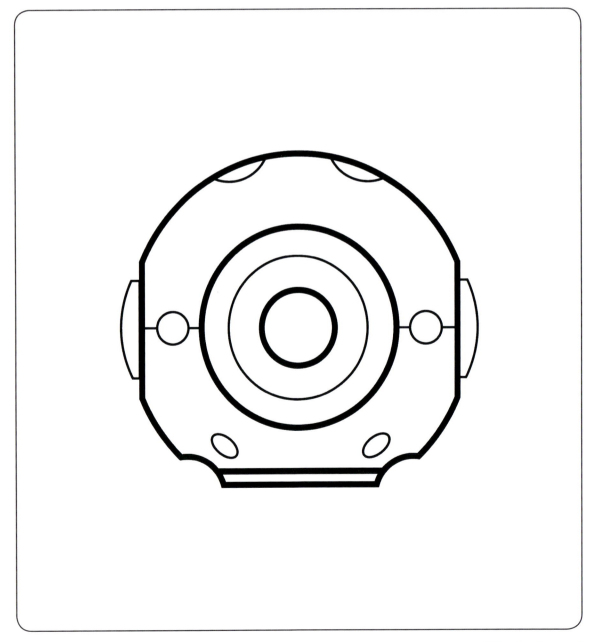

General Planning Worksheet

Name(s): _____   Date: _____

Coding Level: _____   Card #: _____

1. What do you want Dash or Dot to do?

Draw out the steps of the challenge or write a few sentences describing your goal.

2. What will you do to achieve your solution?

What will each team member do? What steps will you need to take? What blocks will you use?

Challenge Card Checklist

Name(s): _____

Level A

- ☐ 1.1: Ready, Set, Go!
- ☐ 1.2: Ready, Set, Dance!
- ☐ 1.3: Ready, Set, Rainbow!
- ☐ 2.1: Smile, Dot!
- ☐ 2.2: Dot Count Down
- ☐ 2.3: Dot's Surprise!
- ☐ 2.4: Dash Saves the Day!
- ☐ 2.5: Dash the Guard
- ☐ 2.6: Dash Guards Again!
- ☐ 3.1: The Forever Light Show
- ☐ 3.2: Dance, Dash, Dance!
- ☐ 3.3: Dash Guards a Lot!

Level B

- ☐ 1.1: Dash the Collector
- ☐ 1.2: It's Candy Time!
- ☐ 1.3: Egg Help!
- ☐ 2.1: Petting Zoo
- ☐ 2.2: Quick, Hide!
- ☐ 2.3: You Are Getting Sleepy
- ☐ 2.4: Littered Lake
- ☐ 2.5: Recycling Rush
- ☐ 2.6: Dash's Trash
- ☐ 3.1: On Your Mark!
- ☐ 3.2: Get Set!
- ☐ 3.3: Go, Go, Go!

Challenge Card Checklist

Name(s): _____

Level C

- ☐ 1.1: No Homework!
- ☐ 1.2: Come Back!
- ☐ 1.3: Wait!
- ☐ 2.1: Connect the Dots
- ☐ 2.2: The Dot Show
- ☐ 2.3: It's Your Turn!
- ☐ 2.4: Sleepy Time
- ☐ 2.5: Wake Up!
- ☐ 2.6: Lights Out!
- ☐ 3.1: Spaceship Spinout!
- ☐ 3.2: Help, help, help!
- ☐ 3.3: Robot Rescue!

Level D

- ☐ 1.1: Cheer Up, Friends!
- ☐ 1.2: Step It Up!
- ☐ 1.3: Happy Dance Flash Mob!
- ☐ 2.1: Follow the Coach
- ☐ 2.2: Training Day
- ☐ 2.3: The Big Event!
- ☐ 3.1: Fire Monster!
- ☐ 3.2: Big and Scary!
- ☐ 3.3: Curious Fire Monster
- ☐ 3.4: The Dot Monster
- ☐ 3.5: Dash's Escape!
- ☐ 3.6: Dash Escapes Again

Challenge Card Checklist

Name(s): _____

Level E

☐ 1.1: Rootin' Tootin' Line Dance!

☐ 1.2: Dance Along with Dot!

☐ 1.3: Dance Machine Dash!

☐ 2.1: Follow the Leader

☐ 2.2: GOAAAAAL!!!

☐ 2.3: Ready or Not!

☐ 3.1: Dance Rehearsal

☐ 3.2: Fancy Wheelwork

☐ 3.3: Dance Off!

☐ 3.4: Dog Trainer

☐ 3.5: Tricks Galore!

☐ 3.6: Obstacle Course!

Level F

☐ 1.1: Dash-chund

☐ 1.2: Ruff, ruff!

☐ 1.3: Nom, nom, nom!

☐ 2.1: Road Trip!

☐ 2.2: Pump It Up!

☐ 2.3: On the Road!

☐ 3.1: Magic Dot Ball

☐ 3.2: Duck, Dot, Goose!

☐ 3.3: Win, Lose, or Dot!

☐ 3.4: Lucky 7's

☐ 3.5: 13 = Yuck!

☐ 3.6: Black Cats!

Blockly Dash Puzzle Tracker

Name(s): _____

Check off the puzzles that you complete in the Blockly app!

- Driving School
- Dash the Snowman
- Interrupting Robot
- Dash on Planet X
- Police Officer Dash
- Robot Puppy Training
- Ice Skating
- Dance Contest
- Nosy Robot
- Ticking Time Bomb
- The Terrible Troll of Trepidation
- Sleeping Dash Prank
- Farm Animal Noise Machine

178

Blockly Dot Puzzle Tracker

Name(s): _____

Check off the puzzles that you complete in the Blockly app!

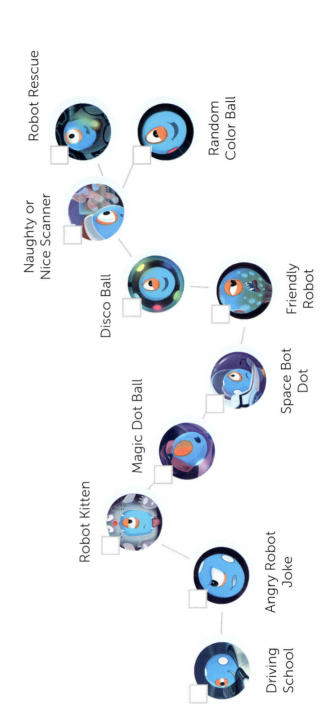

- Robot Rescue
- Random Color Ball
- Naughty or Nice Scanner
- Disco Ball
- Friendly Robot
- Space Bot Dot
- Magic Dot Ball
- Robot Kitten
- Angry Robot Joke
- Driving School

Reflection Worksheet

Name(s): _____ Date: _____

Coding Level: _____ Card #: _____

1. What did Dash and/or Dot do when you ran your program?

2. Did you make any mistakes? If so, how did you fix them?

Advanced Reflection Worksheet

Write a reflection entry in your Wonder Journal. Try to answer these questions as part of your reflection:

Results

- What did Dash and Dot do when you ran your program?

- Did you make any mistakes? If so, how did you fix them?

Connections

- What did you like the most about this challenge? Why?

- What was the most difficult part of the challenge? What did you learn from it?

Next Steps

- If you had more time, how would you change or add to your code?

- What are you planning to do next? Will you try another Challenge Card or start a new coding project?

Troubleshooting

If your program is not running correctly . . .

- Check if Dash and/or Dot are turned on.

- Make sure Dash and/or Dot are connected to the app.

- Make sure your blocks are connected to the **When Start** block.

- Try restarting the app.

If Dash and/or Dot are disconnecting . . .

- Turn off the robots and turn them on again. Then reconnect the robots to the app.

- Press play and then press stop to make the robots reset.

- Try charging the robots.

Three, then me!

- Ask or get help from three of your classmates. If you still need help, then ask the teacher.

Problem Solving & Debugging

Break down the challenge

- What do you need for the challenge? Which robots? Which materials and/or accessories?

- What are Dash and/or Dot supposed to do?

- Have you solved similar challenges to this one?

- Focus on one step at a time.

Plan your solution

- Draw a picture or make a list of what you want Dash or Dot to do.

- What blocks will you need to complete the challenge?

- Are there any hints on the card that can help?

- Use tape to mark Dash's starting point.

- Use tape to mark each obstacle's location.

Test Your Code

- Does your code complete the challenge?

- If not, play your code again. Watch as the program goes through each block. Do you notice any mistakes?

- Do you need to change, delete, or add more blocks?

- Are your blocks telling Dash to do something when you actually want Dot to do something?

Improve your work

- Ask another student or group to check your program.

- Is there an easier way to complete the challenge? Can you use fewer blocks?

- How can you improve your program? Could you add more lights, sounds, or other customizations?

Evaluation Rubric

	Programming	Reflection & Documentation	Collaboration & Communication	Creativity
1 **Novice**	Completed part of the activity and needed assistance throughout the process.	Use a journal, worksheets, and/or multimedia tools (such as video and images) to document some of the activity results.	Participated little or not at all in classroom discussions. Demonstrated little to no cooperation with group members during the activity.	Demonstrated limited creativity in developing ways to complete the activity.
2 **Developing**	Used the targeted coding concept(s) to complete the activity with some assistance.	Incorporated some target vocabulary and some thoughtful reflection on the coding process while documenting activity results using journal entries and multimedia tools.	Occasionally participated in classroom discussions and cooperated somewhat with group members.	Developed a few different ways to complete the activity, but the solution was not particularly creative.
3 **Proficient**	Used the targeted coding concept(s) to complete the activity without assistance.	Incorporated target vocabulary and reflection on the coding process. Clearly documented activity results using journal entries and multimedia tools.	Actively participated in classroom discussions. Answered questions and cooperated with group members during the activity.	Applied the iterative process to develop creative and unexpected solutions for the activity.
4 **Exemplary**	Used the targeted coding concept(s) to complete the activity without assistance. Enhanced the solution with more efficient (e.g., fewer blocks) and/or advanced features (e.g., lights, sounds) in the code.	Incorporated advanced target vocabulary and in-depth reflection on the coding process. Thoroughly and clearly documented and presented activity results.	Actively participated in classroom discussions and cooperated with group members. Gave constructive feedback to others and effectively incorporated feedback from others.	Went above and beyond to develop, revise, and execute imaginative solutions for the activity.

Glossary

- **algorithm**: a sequence of instructions that can be used to solve a problem or set of problems

- **computational thinking**: problem-solving related to computers, programming, or computer science using skills such as decomposing problems, pattern recognition, abstraction, and automation

- **conditional**: instructions that depend on whether something is true or false

- **debugging**: identifying and preventing unintended behavior of a computer or program

- **event**: an interaction or change that can be sensed by a computer or robot

- **event handler**: a program with specific instructions for whenever an event happens

- **function**: a sequence of instructions, usually given a name, that can be reused throughout a program or in other programs

- **function call**: an instruction that executes the sequence of instructions in a function

- **growth mindset**: the belief that one's skills and aptitudes can be developed over time

- **loop**: a set of instructions that repeats either a certain number of times, forever, or until something specific happens

- **nested**: refers to an instruction inside another instruction (e.g., a nested loop is a loop inside of another loop)

- **program**: a sequence of instructions, usually written for a computer

- **sequence**: an arrangement of steps in a specific order to describe a procedure

- **variable**: a name or symbol that represents a number (or some other value) that can be referred to in a program and changed over time